Free Market Fusion

how entrepreneurs and nonprofits create 21st century success

freemarketfusion.com

MarketAbility
Marketing & Public Relations, With a Twist!
813A 14th Street
Golden, CO 80401
303-279-4349

Also By Glenn R. Jones

Cyberschools: An Education Renaissance

Make All America a School

Jones Cable Television and Information Infrastructure Dictionary

Briefcase Poetry Volumes 1-3

Free Market Fusion

how entrepreneurs and nonprofits
create 21st century success

freemarketfusion.com

By Glenn R. Jones

With a foreword by Gary Hart

PUBLISHED BY CYBER PUBLISHING GROUP,™ INC.
Denver, Colorado

Copyright © 1999 by Glenn R. Jones

ISBN 1-885400-68-3

Library of Congress Catalog Card No.: 99-72445

To the entrepreneurs of the 21st century.

About the author

Glenn R. Jones, often referred to as "the poet of technology," purchased his first cable television system in 1967 with $400 borrowed against his Volkswagen. In the following three decades, his company, Jones Intercable,® Inc., became one of the ten largest cable television operators in the United States. Under the aegis of his Jones International,™ Ltd., Mr. Jones has created a number of innovative enterprises, among them, Knowledge TV® Jones International University™: The University of the Web,™ the Global Alliance for Transnational Education® (GATE®), Jones International Networks™ Ltd., Great American Country® (GAC™), Product Information Network® (PIN™), Jones Entertainment Group,™ Ltd., Jones Cyber Solutions,® Ltd., and the Jones Knowledge Group,™ Inc.

Mr. Jones founded Jones International University: The University of the Web, the first fully accredited academic institution created from the ground up for the Internet.

He has served on the board of directors and the executive committee of the National Cable Television Association (NCTA), Cable in the Classroom and C-SPAN, and on the boards of the National Alliance of Business (NAB) and the American Society for Training and Development (ASTD). Mr. Jones has received awards for advancing minorities and women in media. He also has received several honorary doctoral degrees and has been inducted into the Broadcast and Cable Hall of Fame.

Table of Contents

A map of this book

If you purchased an electronic, downloadable version of *Free Market Fusion*, you now have a fully interactive book that will allow you to navigate at will between the Free Market Fusion flow chart, table of contents, chapters, case studies and end notes. Plus, you can utilize various other hyperlinks attached to the illustrations and outside resources.

If you're holding a print version of the book, then the following suggestions may assist you in planning your reading:

- For an immediate overview and understanding of Free Market Fusion, read the Introduction and Chapters 1-3. These chapters include summary references to some of the case studies and practical applications, plus the theory.

- If you are interested in the concept of Free Market Fusion entrepreneurship, but would like more examples, read Chapters 1-5 and the case studies available both here and on the Web site *freemarketfusion.com*. These chapters provide an overall historical context for entrepreneurship, philanthropy, and good pointers on how mavericks have bucked the tide to reach their goals.

- If you are just beginning your quest for a worthwhile cause, but intend to move quickly, it's important to begin some of the scanning process and knowledge database building while you're reading the book. Read Chapters 1,

6, 8, and take the interactive Free Market Fusion Index test described in Chapter 9 and available on the Web site. Read the remaining chapters while you practice your scanning techniques.

- If you already have identified a nonprofit or other organization's mission with which to begin a partnership, use the key elements of Stage 1 on the flow chart at the front of the book by reading Chapters 1 and 6-8. This will help you put your plan of action into effect as quickly as possible. You may read the other chapters at your leisure.

- If you know what you want to do, the Entrepreneur's Tool Kit in Chapters 6-9, dealing with scanning and building a knowledge database, scenario planning, and rules of the game, can be put to immediate use.

- If you are already fully engaged in a Free Market Fusion-style of enterprise, but would like some guidance, or the organization would like to prepare itself fully for seeking more resources and investment, engage in Stage 2 on the flow chart at the front of the book, which entails putting Chapters 6-8 to work.

Foreword

As he has pioneered using technology to build bridges between private sector business and popularly-available education, so Glenn Jones here pioneers in seeking to fuse the separate strengths of creative private entrepreneurship with public institution stability to release a new dynamic into the economies of a new century and millennium.

Almost a half century ago, the British social observer C. P. Snow acknowledged and sought also to bridge a then growing gap between science and the humanities. We are still struggling with that gap, as evidenced by proliferation of weapons of mass destruction and the struggle of the discipline of ethics to keep pace with cloning and genetic manipulation. Glenn Jones implicitly perceives the gap between information technology "haves" and "have nots" and the window of opportunity now open to information entrepreneurs to close that gap.

His answer in this book is to harness the explosively expanding new knowledge engines to the community agenda to make knowledge, the new generator of economic growth and opportunity, as widely available and as specifically applicable as possible.

Glenn Jones advocates new business models and management styles. He focuses special attention on three critical social sectors: electronic democracy; environmentally sustainable growth; and the human agenda of education, poverty, and health. He is particularly concerned with the fissure between information and knowledge.

The author punctuates each of six chapters with pithy, interesting interviews with knowledge leaders and pioneers. His principal chapters include: the free market fusion thesis; convergence; the impact of change; coping with change; entrepreneurs as inventors; scanning as a fusion tool; scenario building; then the rules of the fusion game and a free market fusion index. His distinguished stable of interviewees include: Alvin and Heidi Toffler; Richard Saul Wurman; David Osborne; James Fallows; Andrew Garvin; and Theodore Modis. Glenn Jones has the rare willingness to test his own theses on some top minds in the knowledge transformation game.

Unlike too many business people, and as the self-proclaimed disciple of Friedmanite *laissez faire*, the author is willing to acknowledge an occasional "entrepreneurial" role for government. As the jet engine, developed for the national defense, later stimulated and revolutionized commercial air travel, so the Internet, developed by and for the U.S. national laboratory network, has become an even greater dynamo for economic revolution. Rather than engage in the too-frequent practice of condemning any and all government activity, Glenn Jones recognizes that public institutions offer stable organizational structures and reaffirm a sense of community.

Schumpeter's "destructive gales of change" are upon us, as the author notes, and he advocates an original and creative formula to harness these gales for the common good. He finds the secular text for his thesis in the founder Thomas Jefferson: "...laws and institutions must go hand in hand with the progress of the human mind." No one has yet made the case for reform as the means of conservation better.

No better introduction to this important new book can be given than the author's own words. In *Free Market Fusion*, Glenn Jones writes:

"While clearly we cannot control change, we can, through our commitment to life-enhancing policies and choices, attempt to orchestrate its movement...In order to direct this future, however, we must learn how to balance the competing demands of stewardship versus growth, community versus diversity, people versus profits, and government versus the private sector. There is no reason to assume that in the future these considerations cannot be complementary."

Gary Hart
Kittredge, Colorado
February, 1999

Acknowledgements

Measuring the differences between entrepreneurial pursuits in the aggressive business arena and the endeavors of nonprofit enterprises, and examining how the two can profitably converge, has been a challenging experience. It would have been nigh well impossible without the help of numerous individuals who have shared their thoughts, creativity, personal anecdotes, and criticisms during the nine years this book has been a work in progress.

First, my sincere thanks to Alvin and Heidi Toffler whose willingness to reflect on societal changes not only added a new dimension to *Free Market Fusion*'s historical context, but led me to seek out other authorities willing to be interviewed. Richard Saul Wurman, David Osborne, James Fallows, Andrew Garvin, and Theodore Modis shared their thoughts on a wide range of current management, economic, political and social paradigms and phenomena. Their comments serve as a litmus test, against which the ideas expressed in each chapter can be judged by the reader.

My thanks to Kim Dority and Erica Stull, whose early support many years ago helped me shape the concepts and philosophy of *Free Market Fusion*, and for their critical reviews of the manuscript in its final stages. Special thanks to Jim Sample for his research, polishing and editing of the many drafts of the book over its final three years of preparation and for organizing and spearheading the editing and publishing efforts.

A special acknowledgement and thanks to Dr. James Billington, Librarian of Congress, whose initial invitation to assist the Library in its digitization efforts led me to focus on the entrepreneurial dynamic required for such undertakings. He also offered his comments and observations on the field of information research, helping me to form a better understanding of the importance of such undertakings for entrepreneurial endeavors.

Special thanks for professional editing, fact-checking and proofing to Constance Hardesty and Missy Grealy, who responded to tight deadlines with aplomb and extremely helpful recommendations. Debbie Agnew, Maria Boeding, Kelly Swindell, Michael Moore and Brian Scott provided superb design and typesetting skills, while Karen Polaski literally translated sketches from the backs of paper napkins into professional graphics to illustrate the book's main concepts and processes.

Finally, my thanks to the many associates and friends within the Jones group of companies who have shared their ideas and energies with me over the past 35 years. Their efforts to provide exemplary service, quality and understanding in their jobs and in their endeavors as volunteers is a testimonial to what *Free Market Fusion* can provide at the individual level. I am indebted to them all.

Introduction

I love the new economy and the fast-paced cyber-age companies that are its fundamental DNA. It may come as somewhat of a surprise, then, that I think many of those companies won't survive the next decade.

Why? Because the biggest revenue generators of the cyber-economy are based on organizational models that are over 50 years old. They are organized on slightly-skewed models of automobile assembly lines, with computer engineering terminals replacing electric wrenches and groups of code-writers spewing out building blocks of 0s and 1s to fill out the season's 4.0 product release.

If this is September, it must be time for the newest upgrade, just like the family bought a new Chevy or Ford every three years in the 1950s and 1960s.

"But it works so well," the proponents argue.

Perhaps, for awhile. But such business models don't begin to reflect the real advantage of our new technologies, nor the minds and aspirations of the 20- and 30-year-old engineers and operators who make them successful. They want challenge; they embrace chaos; the freedom of creativity is their short-term goal. As Peter Drucker wrote recently, the popular basics of management have outlived their time, and this applies to entrepreneurship and the fundamentals of starting new enterprises in the 21st century as well.

Likewise, the nature of philanthropy is changing. The giving of wealth is about to be greatly augmented and perhaps partially replaced with giving of expertise, ideas, and enthusiasm.

Free Market Fusion is a new way to practice enlightened business start-ups and fulfill what were once philanthropic missions. It reflects my personal experience and my personal observations of several key business trends and developments.

I am a firm believer in the basic tenets of *laissez faire* economics and principles, and a disciple of the Milton Friedman school of free market thought. Friedman, who has spent his adult life championing the application of human capital and efficacy of free markets, has helped create the economic environment in which examples of Free Market Fusion can proliferate.[1] However, in this book I aim to pose and explain a simple, straight-forward approach to entrepreneurship, leaving economic theory to the experts.

A primer for entrepreneurs

This is a primer, or handbook, based on real life experiences and the school of hard knocks. It is intended for entrepreneurs, both in the private and nonprofit sectors, who are willing to recognize the importance of converging the resources and talents inherent in both private and nonprofit approaches to providing services and goods to the benefit of a market society's evolution.

Considering this objective, the reader may wonder why a portion of this book is devoted to a review and discussion of business and communication history and change. The reason is straightforward: Successful implementation of a Free Market Fusion process requires managers and leaders to understand what the future may hold beyond immediate accomplishment of quarterly or annual objectives, be those objectives immediate financial returns or test marketing of products and services. In today's market, the successful leader must be a visionary. To be a visionary and enhance one's odds of succeeding in a risk-prone world, it helps to be a student of history. As the philosopher George Santayana cautioned, "Those who cannot remember the past are condemned to repeat it."[2]

What is Free Market Fusion?

As defined in Chapter 1, Free Market Fusion is an entrepreneurial approach to identifying or creating opportunities for innovative solutions. It involves for-profit and nonprofit enterprises.

There are many examples of Free Market Fusion, and a number have been selected for the case studies which appear as companions to the book chapters. The topics with which I have had some firsthand experience include certain library projects which have led to the digitization of large numbers of books, maps and documents including those that are considered national treasures of the countries involved. These projects were undertaken with instrumental initial funding by private companies at a time when diminishing tax-supported funding had raised the specter of permanent loss.

The offering by private companies of for-credit college courses, first on TV and later on the Internet, began at a time when interest had waned in both the public and private sectors in the delivery of distance education college courses and programs via electronic means. Now, in 1999, virtual universities are being heralded by some as a solution for the tidal wave of escalating college costs in the U.S. and for the severe classroom shortages in other countries.

The topics chosen for case studies in this book and some which will be forthcoming at *freemarketfusion.com* cover a diverse area of interests. Included are the National Digital Library project at the Library of Congress, build-operate-transfer (BOT) public infrastructure projects, appropriate small-scale technology applications for farmers and handcraft workers in developing countries, a unique public charter school in Detroit, Michigan that operates in partnership with Ford Motor Co., and the rapid building of the Asian Internet.

The World Wide Web as Free Market Fusion

This book not only documents experiments in Free Market Fusion, it is an ongoing experiment itself. It is concurrently being published in print and in electronic, downloadable form via a World Wide Web site on the Internet. It has both formal marketing relationships and a symbiotic relationship with other Web publishing ventures, including the highly popular Internet book store amazon.com, and various education and publishing sites and directories through which on-line researchers can reach *freemarketfusion.com.*

Many organizations and products on the Web represent forms of Free Market Fusion in that they are delivered through technology that is still developing.

In fact, the Internet was spawned by public funding, then reached a point where it was attractive to and needed private backing. The Free Market Fusion process occurred when government could no longer afford the cost of expanding the Internet and its underlying infrastructure. That event happened to coincide with the emergence of ubiquitous private sector technology in the form of affordable Internet servers, browsers, fast modems and powerful multimedia computers. The result was Free Market Fusion: A universal access global Internet was born. Both public and private sectors will share in the long-term rewards.

This book does not treat the global phenomenon of the Internet as a case study because it is already the topic of so much in-depth study and research.

I invite readers to view it as an interactive experiment in both business strategy and delivery of a product. Those who wish to comment on the contents or engage in electronic discussion may do so by using the e-mail address at the end of this introduction. Suggestions for additional case studies are welcome.

This book is, above all, a tool kit. The reader should employ the enclosed implements in the handiest, most effective way, regardless of the traditional organization and table of contents.

Meanwhile, please enjoy this interactive book, and good luck in your Free Market Fusion endeavors.

Glenn R. Jones
February, 1999
gjones@freemarketfusion.com

CHAPTER 1

FREE MARKET FUSION

A new entrepreneurial approach

What is Free Market Fusion? It is an entrepreneurial approach to identifying or creating opportunities for innovative solutions.

In chemical terms, fusion occurs when two elements combine to create different elements and, simultaneously, release a tremendous amount of energy. Fusion is one of the most powerful processes known; physicists around the world race to find a means to safely harness its potential.

Free Market Fusion is both a process and its result. It is a process that creates new products, services or solutions and is associated with new or highly modified management concepts and organizational goals. Entire industries or portions of them can be involved and the mix of participants can range widely.

Free Market Fusion is the coming together of two or more entities, one or more of which is characterized as a for-profit enterprise and one or more of which is characterized as an institutional, nonprofit, quasi-governmental, or government entity. For purposes of illustration, we'll call them *A entities* (for-profit) and *B entities* (institutional, nonprofit, etc.). The process culminates in the fusing of some, or possibly all, of the assets of one or more A entities with some or all of the assets of one or more B entities (see Figure 1).

Figure I

FREE MARKET FUSION PROCESS

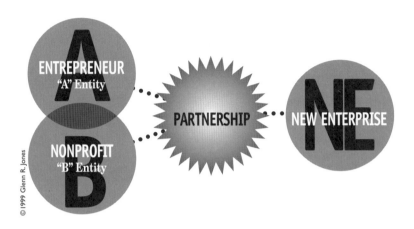

This relationship can be further illustrated as shown in the large (fold-out) process diagram, Figure 2, appearing on page 11.

Although Free Market Fusion may result in the formation of new enterprises, typically at the outset existing organizations are the creators. Also, typically there is a background of significant common need, concern, or opportunity relative to the entities involved that generates support for resolution. At its ideal, the collaborative process inherent in Free Market Fusion can engender the tremendous release of energies that comes from looking at the world not as a miasma of intractable problems, but as an arena of challenges awaiting exploration, initiative, resolution, and reward.

How Free Market Fusion Works

In the Free Market Fusion process, each entity contributes its particular strengths to the project. For example, in a partnership between an entrepreneurial group or individual and an institution, the entrepreneur can contribute the initial innovative idea as well as technological and marketing expertise, significant risk assumption, and free market disciplines such as accountability to shareholders and competitive strategy. The institution can contribute staff resources, physical facilities, familiarity with the existing market, credibility, and stature.

Depending on the parties, some of the roles might be reversed. However, the purpose of the partnership is always to enable both parties to accomplish goals each would find difficult to attain alone — to create a new solution where seemingly there was none. As in a fusion process, that new solution is accompanied by a burst of energy as new possibilities and opportunities open up to everyone involved in the process, both those creating the solution and those benefiting from it.

The strengths of the entrepreneur should include expertise in competitive strategies and the ability to evaluate and undertake appropriate risks. A commitment to innovative thinking, an awareness of opportunities presented by recent technological advances, strategic networking abilities, and an understanding of capital resources, also are important strengths.

The catalyst ingredient is leadership, the "champion." While some may be quick to reach the conclusion that leadership will be provided by the "freewheeling" entrepreneur, this is not always the case. Although an entrepreneur may be accustomed to operating in the public spotlight and in a robust competitive arena, this does not necessarily mean that person will, or should, assume the leadership mantle.

At the same time, leadership encompasses much more than just assuming the role of primary public spokesperson. The most critical leadership activities are planning, organizing, networking, and acting as missionary within the organizations involved, persuading and recruiting supporters internally for a new concept. Often individuals with established credibility within an institution can do this most effectively if they are passionate about the project. The entrepreneur may assume some or most of this role, or merely advise and be an "outside" networker, promoting the concept to other organizations and individuals whose support is essential. This requires a special breed, an arguably "new" brand of entrepreneur whose motivation to make a social contribution resides on the same pedestal with making a profit and wielding influence.

Entrepreneurs and institutions provide an especially effective example of Free Market Fusion. The combination enables the entrepreneur's core strengths (creativity, risk analysis and assumption, aggressiveness, competitive discipline) and the institution's core strengths (including existing facilities, expertise, and reputation) to succeed or exceed together at what neither could achieve alone.

Institutions and Philanthropy

Free Market Fusion is not philanthropy, because it usually leads to a self-sustaining market model. However, the spirit of Free Market Fusion was largely sparked by the legacy of American, British, and European philanthropists helping institutions.

Institutions are a critical part of society's infrastructure. They include schools, colleges and universities, hospitals, prisons, the military services, national charitable organizations, unions and professional organizations, nongovernmental organizations (NGOs), and such community entities as libraries, symphonies, museums, civic leagues, and innumerable religious groups. Often, they have existing physical facilities and a stable organizational structure. Successful institutions have a thorough understanding both of their constituencies and of those constituencies' special needs and concerns.

Our institutions play an important part in reaffirming and continuing a sense of community when we are deluged with an onslaught of change on such a regular basis. As connections to our past, they are familiar and comforting. Some have been in existence longer than the country itself, while others grew with the needs of our growing nation. For example, Harvard was established in 1636, Yale in 1701, and the 1862 Morrill Act fueled the expansion of the public higher education system. Today, the U.S. has some 3,700 institutions of higher learning.

Another institution, the public library, has an equally impressive history. Early American lending libraries were founded by English clergyman Thomas Bray in colonies from Rhode Island to Carolina in the late 1600s, and the U.S.'s public library system was boosted nationally when Andrew Carnegie funded the construction of 1,679 community library buildings in more than 1,400 communities between 1886 and 1917. Today, communities support some 9,000 public libraries across the U.S.

The Boy Scout and Girl Scout programs, which originated in the United Kingdom, serve as yet another example. The programs were introduced in the U.S. early in the 20th century and now involve well over 18 million children, teens, and adults. The YMCA, with 16 million members in more than 130 countries, has been a pillar of thousands of communities since its inception in London in 1844. Additionally, towns and cities across the country have relied upon community hospitals ever since Philadelphia's Pennsylvania Hospital first received its charter in 1751 through the efforts of Dr. Thomas Bond and Benjamin Franklin. The list of public initiatives and institutions spawned or nurtured by the fusion of private and public sector resources and combined management skills is indeed extensive.

Certainly our institutions have played a central role in advancing the goals of society throughout our history.

It is imperative, however, that they remain as vital
and forward thinking as possible, if they are to continue
their positive impact on society. This is no easy task: it
is in the nature of institutions (and of monopolistic
businesses) that stability may deteriorate to stagnation
and management to mediocrity. Thomas Jefferson
recognized this possibility, when he wrote:

> "I am certainly not an advocate for frequent and
> untried change in laws and constitutions...but...
> laws and institutions must go hand in hand
> with the progress of the human mind. As that
> becomes more developed, more enlightened, as
> new discoveries are made, new truths disclosed
> and manners and opinions change with the
> change of circumstances, institutions must
> advance also and to keep pace with the times.
> We might as well require a man to wear still
> the coat which fitted him when a boy, as
> civilized society to remain ever under the regimen
> of their barbarous ancestors."[3]

The tendency of institutions and large organizations
to rely on solutions drawn from yesterday's realities was
pointed out two decades ago by Peter Drucker in his
book, *Management:*

> "...no success lasts "forever." Yet it is even more
> difficult to abandon yesterday's success than it
> is to reappraise a failure. A once successful
> project gains an air of success that outlasts the
> project's real usefulness and disguises its
> failings. In a service institution particularly,
> yesterday's success becomes 'policy,' 'virtue,'
> 'conviction,' if not holy writ. The institution
> must impose on itself the discipline of thinking
> through its mission, its objectives, and its
> priorities, and of building in feedback control
> from results and performance on policies,

priorities, and action. Otherwise, it will gradually become less and less effective."[4]

Our institutions form the infrastructure that undergirds the vitality of America's dreams, growth, and progress. We cannot afford to have our institutions represent the weakest link in our democratic republic. In these times, their quick response is especially important, given the rapidly changing requirements faced by citizens.

Risk Taking: A Key Role

One complementary relationship that can develop between entrepreneurs and partnering institutions relates to risk taking. Often, missteps within an institutional environment may easily spell the end of a promising career, a circumstance that has an obvious and understandable dampening effect on an institutional leader's willingness to take risks. In addition to identifying opportunities, then, another of the entrepreneur's key roles in a Free Market Fusion venture is to assume a substantial amount of the risk involved in any new undertaking. This diverts a large measure of the "exposure" from the institution and its leader onto the entrepreneur.

This imposes no hardship, for although risk-taking is anathema to an institution, judicious and well-informed risk-taking is second nature to the entrepreneur. An entrepreneur has the freedom to respond to opportunity with a desire for gain, rather than resisting it because of a fear of loss. Similarly, because entrepreneurs may not be part of the "old guard" operating environment of the institution, and will have less vested interest in conforming to established ideologies, they are much freer to think outside the bounds of accepted practices and to envision radical alternatives and innovative solutions. It is something they are accustomed to doing, often with outstanding results. In fact, a 1998 major study by MIT business economist David Birch found that small, entrepreneur-led businesses created two-thirds of gross new jobs and all net new jobs in America. Creating jobs is one of the most useful contributions any enterprise can make. This is not a new phenomenon, nor an anomaly. In a 1987 study of job creation, Birch found similar results.[5]

When Thomas Jefferson said "a little rebellion, now and then, is a good thing," he wasn't talking about bloody revolution so much as a strong effort to break away from the constricting ways of the past. Every generation, Jefferson said, should rule itself, tossing out laws and ways of doing things that had outlived their usefulness. Such revolutions would "break the congealing shapes of institutions before they petrified, and thus...leave society free to follow its natural laws of development." To Jefferson, revolution was about more than political tyranny; revolution was a way of "affirming every generation's right to be preserved from old models."

Jefferson's vision of revolution plays itself out every day in free markets. Entrepreneurs have always been society's revolutionaries, operating outside the boundaries, and creating new solutions for a changing world. Now, they have an opportunity to chart new ground once again.

Free Market Fusion can enable aspiring entrepreneurs to build on their unique strengths toward one ultimate goal: to engage all of society's resources — human, financial, physical, and technological — in the creation and support of a free, productive, diverse society. Free Market Fusion provides an opportunity to channel our entrepreneurial contributions in a truly significant manner.

Modeling Free Market Fusion

The major stages of a Free Market Fusion process are (see Figure 2, page 11):

Stage 1. — Mission Research and Selection: Identifying opportunities and needs through scanning and knowledge building

Stage 2. — Planning and Agreements: Evolving innovative solutions and structuring partnerships

Stage 3. — Key Actions: Carrying out the mission

Stage 4. — Outcome Assessment: Going forward or phasing out

Stage I — Mission Research and Selection

The research portion of this step is critical, especially scanning and building a knowledge base to support a current project. Research will not only help the management group with its awareness of key trends and events that may begin to affect the project, but also

>
10

STAGE 4
Outcome Assessment

STAGE 1
Mission Research

ACCOMPLISHED • • •

Mission fulfilled,
enterprise
phased out

Experience added
to knowledge base

**GLOBAL
INTELLIGENCE** • • •

Scan for
opportunities
begins

**KNOWLEDGE
BASE** • • • •

Development of
knowledge base

DEVELOPED • • •

Enterprise
developed as
for-profit

**ROGRESS
SSESSED**

ogress
ward
ssion
iewed,
g-term
oals
usted

MAINTAINED • • •

Partnership
continues

Free Market Fusion
enterprise continues

TRANSFERRED ○ ○ ○

Enterprise
transferred back
to nonprofit

TRADITIONAL ELECTION PROCESS

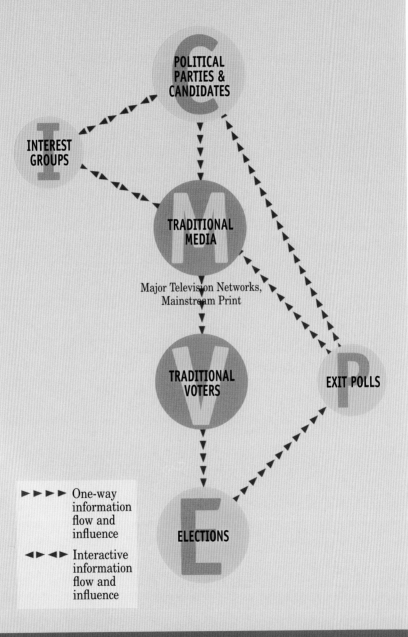

POLITICAL PARTIES & CANDIDATES

INTEREST GROUPS

TRADITIONAL MEDIA

Major Television Networks, Mainstream Print

TRADITIONAL VOTERS

EXIT POLLS

ELECTIONS

►►►► One-way information flow and influence

◄►◄► Interactive information flow and influence

© 1999 Glenn R. Jones

Figure 3 *Repeated on page 20*

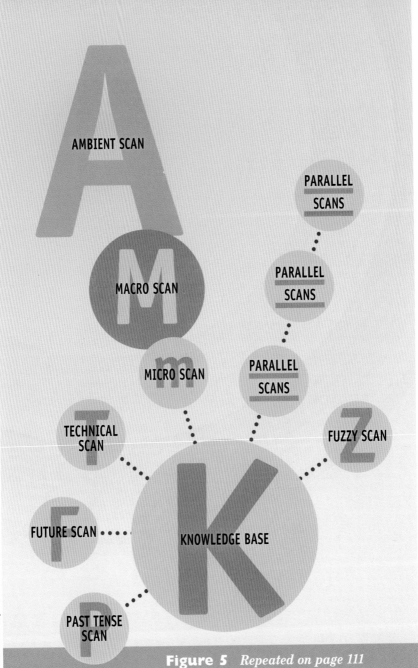

AMBIENT SCAN

PARALLEL SCANS

MACRO SCAN

PARALLEL SCANS

MICRO SCAN

PARALLEL SCANS

TECHNICAL SCAN

FUZZY SCAN

FUTURE SCAN

KNOWLEDGE BASE

PAST TENSE SCAN

Figure 5 *Repeated on page 111*

Figure 2

FREE MARKET FUSION

STAGE 1
Mission Research & Selection

"A" Entity
Search for
mission begins

GLOBAL INTELLIGENCE

Scan for
opportunities
begins

KNOWLEDGE BASE

Development of
knowledge base

POSSIBILITIES IDENTIFIED

Analysis of
options
begins

SCENARIO PLANNING

Planning with
industry experts

"B" Entity
Nonprofit partner with
appropriate mission
identified early

The Process & The Result

STAGE 2	STAGE 3
Planning & Agreements	Key Actions

MISSION

Selection
made

**SCENARIO
PLANNING**

Planning
with partners

**STRATEGIC
PLANS
FINALIZED**

Includes:
• Mission statement
• Financial resources
• Operations detail
• Partnership roles
• Long-term goals

**NEW
ENTERPRISE**

Partnership
established

ACTION

Mission
pursued

INTERACTIVE ELECTION PROCESS

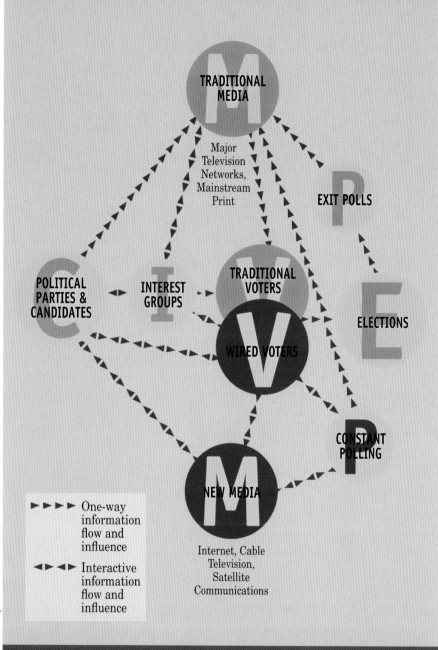

Figure 4 *Repeated on page 21*

it may set the stage for related projects. Building this knowledge base is the topic of Chapter 6, and that process permeates all the processes and steps partners go through as they lay out their objectives and pursue a mission.

Stage 2 — Planning and Agreements

Once a concept of a Free Market Fusion combination is developed, the manner in which these entities and related functions, equipment, personnel, or activities can be joined in appropriate ways must then be considered. What are the costs? Who must contribute what? Who might feel threatened? Who will manage the process? How do we keep the excitement level up? What kind of time frame will it take for Free Market Fusion to function? What are the risks involved and who will take them? Can a self-sustaining financial model be constructed? The list of potential questions to be answered is long, and will vary with each project.

Scenario planning, as explained in Chapter 7, is an important step to galvanize the planning process.

Obviously, each project will have its own set of circumstances and concerns that need to be addressed and agreed upon before other steps can be taken. However, the following areas can serve as a starting point.

Goal issues. What broad opportunity or problem is addressed? What are the specific purposes and goals of this project? How will goals be measured? How and when will they be evaluated?

Inertia issues. Best-laid plans can easily be derailed by organizational inertia. How rapidly will both parties be able to respond to opportunities and/or crises? How rapidly are both parties willing to respond?

Structural and logistics issues. How will the project be undertaken? Where and how will it be located? (Centralized with one participant? Headquartered at a project site? Other?) Who will implement what aspects of the project?

Timing is critical. What is a reasonable and mutually agreeable time frame? This can become a key issue if both parties do not understand and accept how long it will take to accomplish key tasks. If the project will entail working with large institutions, government agencies, or other bureaucracies, the standing rule that everything will take twice as long as predicted might be expanded exponentially. But if the leaders fail to understand and commit to the importance of speed, including allowing for new processes and fast communications, the project may never succeed.

Long-term issues. Assuming the project is successful in meeting its goals and is profitable, what should become of it in the long-term? Should the relationship between the participants continue as is, or should it be reviewed on a specified basis? Should the project continue in its current form or be taken over by one of the participants? Should it be taken public as an established company? Should it move into other Free Market Fusion arenas?

Competition issues. How will the leaders deal with competing players? Will they work around their competitors' established programs, trying not to disturb their "market share," and excite them, or try to displace their competitors' "product" with their own?

When dealing with societal concerns, much care must be taken around this issue. Society is rarely damaged when, in the rough-and-tumble competitive consumer market, a candy bar, laundry detergent, or software program bites the dust. On the other hand, institutional damage could have serious consequences.

Stage 3 — Key Actions

Every situation will demand different levels of time and energy in the action phase. Identifying and acting on these steps might be easy to plan. But this is the phase most likely to derail the project when management styles and groups try to merge. However, if participants know going into an undertaking that there is a process to work through, then resources can be allocated accordingly.

If an innovative solution incorporates a fairly non-traditional concept, it will be easier to work with a partner who already is comfortable with the non-traditional concept. For example, a group of my companies combined non-traditional delivery processes (cable television, satellites, computers, and the Internet) with nontraditional teaching methods using highly adaptive and affordable software on an Internet platform. We found a university that was willing to become our partner to develop a virtual degree program with a masters in business administration program.

Another consideration is that many potential partners may be constrained by people or organizations whose vested interests might be "threatened" by the entity's move into a new arena or into a relationship with another autonomous entity where the vested interests have less control. A major contributor to the organization, for example, may forbid it from entering into any new relationship for fear that the contributor will lose control of the organization's goals and direction.

This is a fairly predictable response. Fear of change is a familiar reaction, especially for constituencies, such as labor unions or government bureaucracies, that have vested interests which are now vulnerable. Therefore it becomes critical to achieve a level of friction that is acceptable, where even though fear of change may be present, it is counterbalanced by enthusiastic commitment to the opportunity at hand.

Stage 4 — Outcome Assessment

This is the step most likely to be omitted or to be replaced by a "mission accomplished" celebration. It is a step that is vital for every project, whether a success or failure. Some sage once quipped that behind every success is the sum total of the leader's failures in life. Interestingly, it is the success that is the most difficult to assess. We are so inclined to focus on everything that went right, and the sheer brilliance and good luck of the team, that the near-disasters and what lay beyond the second fork in the road that we didn't take are forgotten quickly. It is these elements that form the most important lessons we take away from a mission, and that can serve us best when the next opportunity comes along.

Outcome assessment should take place in the first few weeks after a mission's objective has been attained. If the mission is to continue, then it will be a natural part of on-going planning. If the mission group has worked itself out of a job, then schedule a meeting to do the assessment as early as possible before the team members leave for other pursuits.

The essentials of the outcome assessment are to block out a half day or a day to assemble the team, then bring in a group facilitator who knows about the project but hasn't been involved in its activities. If possible, make an audio or video tape of the session, and designate the facilitator and at least one team member to write a lessons-learned report. This not only will provide an important addition to the knowledge base that has been building since Stage 1, but also will help bring positive closure to the involvement of the team members.

New Areas for Free Market Fusion

There are many areas where Free Market Fusion approaches are currently or will soon enable us to make more creative, effective use of the technological tools now available. Several examples are included in case studies as well, but key areas to examine for opportunities include:

Electronic democracy. The 1990s will be known as the decade when we began to see the potential for electronic democracy.

The two "entities" in this case can be considered the American democratic election system and international communications and information entrepreneurs.

The catalyst for change came from the opportunities created by America's entrepreneurial electronic/ telecommunications/information companies. This composite entity comprised cable and satellite television, advanced telephone services, computers, and the Internet. Cable networks and the Internet in particular brought about the instant distribution of information from polling and survey organizations, plus analysis from a proliferation of pundits representing an enormous range of points of view across the political and social spectrums. Of course, television and radio had the "instant" option available for years, but elected not to use it except on rare occasions. Such applications of technology present a very fresh perspective on the "flow chart" of the media/political process (see pages 20 and 21).

In this new arena of electronic campaigning, lobbying, and voting, there is a decided overlap with many facets of electronic commerce that have evolved within the Internet and TV industries as of early 1999. But the new model for making money looks more like a game of 8-ball pool than the old flow-through, top-down process of controlling information, and buying and selling licenses and program fees. "Follow the money" is a tried and true method of deciphering a successful business process, but when it comes to electronic politics and government, dropping the right ball in the pocket may require a two, three or even four cushion shot, weaving through a labyrinth of obstacles.

The small Internet consulting companies that didn't even exist in the mid-1990s might make profits immediately. There also are opportunities for cable networks and Internet marketing companies that understand how to reach niche audiences and political constituencies that are wired for the new media. These, in turn, offer the opportunity for nonprofit groups and lobbyists to join with them in "virtual" partnerships to carry out campaigns, developing fresh demographic and political data and analysis. These groups can in turn sell their new knowledge databases back to a myriad of traditional and new customers, including political parties, campaigns and consultants, the major TV and radio networks, and other new media groups and startups hungry for effective ways to reach active, savvy Internet customers.

Figure 3

TRADITIONAL ELECTION PROCESS

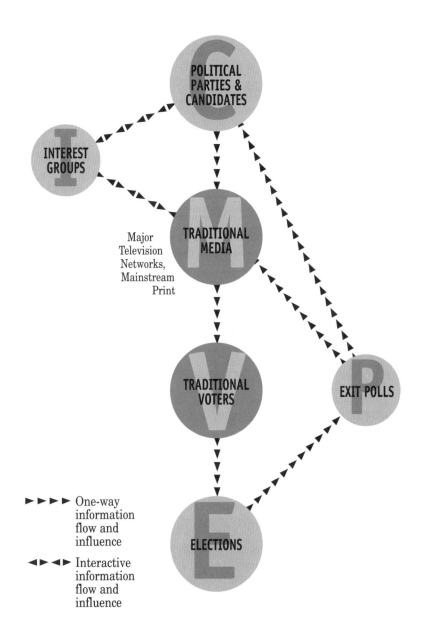

POLITICAL PARTIES & CANDIDATES

INTEREST GROUPS

Major Television Networks, Mainstream Print

TRADITIONAL MEDIA

TRADITIONAL VOTERS

EXIT POLLS

►►►► One-way information flow and influence

◄►◄► Interactive information flow and influence

ELECTIONS

Figure 4

INTERACTIVE ELECTION PROCESS

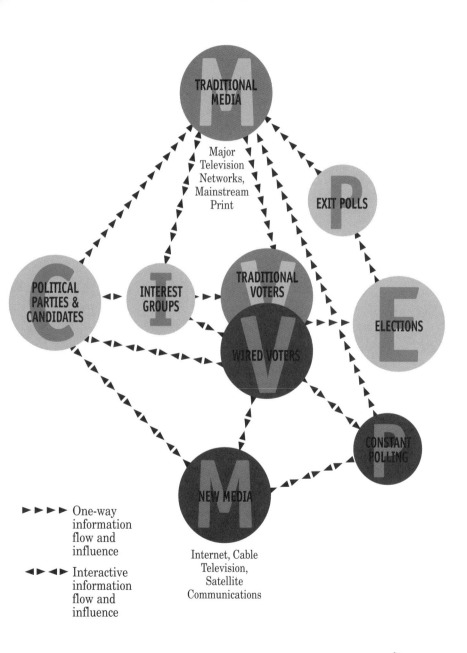

TRADITIONAL
MEDIA

Major
Television
Networks,
Mainstream
Print

EXIT POLLS

POLITICAL
PARTIES &
CANDIDATES

INTEREST
GROUPS

TRADITIONAL
VOTERS

WIRED VOTERS

ELECTIONS

CONSTANT
POLLING

NEW MEDIA

Internet, Cable
Television,
Satellite
Communications

►►►► One-way
information
flow and
influence

◄►◄► Interactive
information
flow and
influence

Through the Free Market Fusion process, combining the assets of one entity (the electronic/ telecommunications/information industry) with the assets and strengths of another (the American democratic political system), a new solution can be created: an electronic democracy to address society's need for a more participative, voter-empowered democracy.

Environment. Some 30 years have passed since the first Earth Day in April 1970 called the world's attention to the deteriorating state of the global environment. Since that first tolling bell of warning, we have become increasingly familiar with the challenges that confront us, including global warming, ozone depletion, forest depletion, and water resource contamination.

Sustainable development is a goal we all must embrace. It is imperative to accept the fact that market-based environmentalism offers the most effective means of transferring technological advances into the areas of greatest need, ensuring that future generations will inherit a land, not a landfill.

Education, poverty and health. The list of challenges we face is long and daunting. A quick hit list of social concerns might include the high dropout rate for high school minorities, poor skill levels of high school graduates, illiteracy, child poverty, drug addiction, AIDS, homelessness, overcrowded prisons and a sky-high recidivism rate, increasing the level of effectiveness and accessibility (financial as well as logistic) for our higher education resources, re-incorporating seniors, with their skills and experience, into productive societal roles, mainstreaming the physically handicapped back into society, adequate, affordable medical care for all, and providing a competent global workforce.

The world has been caught in a web of suffering that decades of goodwill, foreign aid, and well-intentioned efforts have failed to eradicate. The problems have seemed incapable of solution. Yet are they?

The Larger Arena: Tapping Entrepreneurial Talent

Where do we begin? How do we begin? We can begin with Free Market Fusion.

Why not turn to the world's entrepreneurs and allow them to participate? These are people with the special instincts and training to see the opportunities in change and the possibilities in dislocation. They have fertile imaginations. They are not afraid to play "the hunch."

If the constraints are not too severe, they will focus their energies on markets whether or not there are restrictive governmental structures and regulations. Whether or not the market is monopolistic. And whether or not there are stifling vested interests protecting sacred cows. If the reward is large enough, entrepreneurs will reorder existing resources, re-think current responses, create new solutions, take the risk and attack.

We need to tap the creative energy and risk-taking spirit of those willing to operate in the late information-age visionary Buckminster Fuller's "outlaw area" of untried solutions and no guarantees.

I believe solutions are always possible. The key for us is to structure nurturing, creative circumstances so that our most innovative thinkers can design new solutions. For it is obvious that when a society faces a problem that has continually resisted traditional means of resolution, other solutions must be invented and tried. It becomes necessary to think and create outside the structure of established assumptions and policies. We must gather our most powerful resources and engage the challenges.

CHAPTER 2

CONVERGENCE
Accelerating change and the
need for Free Market Fusion

A key phenomenon that has made possible new entrepreneurship approaches, including Free Market Fusion, has been the proliferation and convergence of new technology. This trend has been both enabling and disquieting.

In 1970, a 42-year-old writer and social critic blazed across the consciousness of America with a frightening, prescient view of the late 20th century. He predicted that the rate of change was accelerating so rapidly that if steps were not taken immediately to slow its pace, society might face massive breakdown.

Alvin Toffler was looking back at the 20 years of transition the U.S. had undergone since 1950, when the country had faced the second half of the century as a cheerily confident, industrialized, homogenous society. As Toffler described his view of late-1960s industrialized society in his best-seller, *Future Shock*:

> New discoveries, new technologies, new social arrangements in the external world erupt into our lives in the form of increased turnover rates— shorter and shorter relational durations. They force a faster and faster pace of daily life. They demand a new level of adaptability. And they set the stage for that potentially devastating social illness—future shock.[6]

Toffler was right, though he and co-author Heidi Toffler were more skeptical of traditional economists in 1998 than they were in 1970[7] (see the interview on page 43). Seemingly every aspect of American life has undergone radical change in the quarter century since *Future Shock* first hit the bookstands. Institutions have felt the wrenching impact of Toffler's "accelerative thrust," as have the assumptions that underlie them. Old alliances are shattering, and new constituencies are rising. Huge vested interests and institutions are stressed to the point of cataclysmic change. Everywhere we look, the global landscape has changed. And every day the change seems to accelerate and become even more intense.

Technology and Societal Change

Arguably, the changes that have been most pervasive and had the greatest acceleration effect on other changes in society are the advances in the field of information storage, manipulation and communication, combined with the convergence of these technologies with the biosciences. While this melding of technology has provoked a storm of controversy, especially surrounding the possibilities of genetic engineering, it nevertheless represents tremendous potential for improving the lot of the planet's species.

Both industrial mankind of the late 19th century and atomic mankind of the mid-20th century have been superseded by bionic man. Despite the anti-cloning furor that arose anew in the spring of 1997, cloning in various manifestations is already upon us. And before cloning, we already had begun a steady extension of the human mind, body, and lifespan, through pacemakers, artificial valves, joints and limbs, and various wireless devices that transmit and receive information the individual needs. In essence, we now behold the evolution of a truly augmented humankind. With electronic devices and connecting membranes such as the Internet, our minds are almost literally linked to millions of data sources. We have become "cyborgs" — electronically-enhanced beings.

This is the platform of change upon which new evolutionary changes will be launched.

The Ubiquitous PC

To appreciate just how far we've come in a very short time, some historical perspective is important.

In 1950, the computer was a mastodon of whirring parts, reliable output, and just a few important applications. The Electrical Numerical Integrator and Computer (ENIAC), was unveiled in 1946 at the University of Pennsylvania by J.P. Eckert and John Mauchly. It was the best-known of the early computers, took up 3,000 cubic feet of space, weighed in at a sturdy 30 tons, comprised 1,000,000 components housed in 40 cabinets (including 18,000 vacuum tubes), and ran on 140 kilowatts of electricity.[8]

No technological slouch, ENIAC improved on the computing speeds of its predecessor, IBM and Harvard University's Mark I, a thousand fold, speeding through 5,000 addition and subtraction, 350 multiplication, or 50 division problems per second. A personal computer was impractical and, to some, ridiculous. In mid-century, IBM president Tom Watson, Sr. observed that there was no reason for any individual to own a computer, and that there would probably never be a need for more than 500 computers in the world at any given time. This seemed a reasonable assumption in the 1950s, but by 1995, more than 35.2 million U.S. households owned one or more personal computers, along with more than 25 million video game players.

By 1970 the storage and computation capacities of the average computer had increased exponentially, but personal computers had grabbed the imagination and checkbooks of only a small cadre of technologically adventurous individuals. However, by 1977, Apple Computers' Apple II had catapulted into the arena as the "Volkswagen of computers," and electronics engineers the world over were starting to realize just how many applications could be found for tiny silicon chips. Seymour Cray was revolutionizing computing technology with his CRAY-I supercomputer, crunching data at a speed of 100 megaflops (or about 100 million "floating-point" operations) per second, and the Japanese electronics industry was leaping into the fray with innovative products designed to push the limits of the advancing technologies.

In the late 20th century, microchips were embedded in so many products that they were rapidly becoming ubiquitous in the same manner as electricity. Their contribution is found in everything from greeting cards, smart cards, and watches to remote-controlled space probes and satellite transmissions. ENIAC's successor, the microprocessor based on the silicon chip, takes up only 0.011 cubic feet, weighs in at .0525 grams, and consumes under 2.5 watts of electricity, less than it takes to power a residential smoke alarm.

Meanwhile, in addition to progress in computing speeds, there has been similar progress in the cost-per-computational-power ratio. In the late 1980s, the memory for computers cost less than one-one-hundred-millionth of what it cost in 1950,[9] and this cost efficiency has increased over the last decade to the point that computer memory is, by some estimates, almost free. Customers now pay largely for its packaging and shipping.

Cyborgs Have Arrived

Even computing at speeds almost a million times faster than ENIAC, however, our fastest computers move slowly compared to the computing ability of the human mind. Experts estimate that the human brain's processing capability is greater than that of 1,000 super computers, with human vision alone requiring 100 trillion computations per second. Meanwhile, the "cyborg" — a computer-augmented human — has quickly made the transition from science fiction and research to reality. In the late 1990s, students, scientists, surgeons, astronauts, and military pilots regularly carried out their professional tasks with computers strapped to their bodies, in order to enhance performance and computations.

Computers revolutionized the workplace. As they have increased in power and steadily shrunk in size, computers have found ready applications in product and parts inventory systems, ensuring precision die-cuts in materials plants, monitoring livestock food additives and quality of individual cow milk production, and around-the-clock analysis of soil conditions for crops. In developed countries, computer chips have become ubiquitous and indispensible in applications ranging from toys to automobile instruments to Mars rover vehicles.

They have made possible the big leap into robotics. In 1970, robotics had more credibility in Saturday morning cartoons than in America's boardrooms. Today, as we move into the fourth generation of robotic technology, there are over 70 U.S. companies specializing in production of robotics and robotic systems integration, with shipments in 1993 of $400 million-$500 million.[10] In fact, industry analysts estimated that between 1983 and 1998, American companies invested more than $30 billion in factory automation and robotics.

We now witness even more impressive gains in computer capacities and broad scale applications every few months, leading to both productivity increases and the necessity for a higher level of worker skills. These new technologies will be resource-efficient in a world of resource shortages. They will substitute the clean, environment-friendly efficiency of computer chips for the waste-producing, environmentally damaging output of fossil fuels. As finite fossil fuels continue to be consumed, computer chips multiply in productivity and availability. And the price drops with every new generation. While the world moves more and more to an information and knowledge-based economy, we will be able to realize major productivity increases, concurrent with environmental damage decreases, by moving materials through computer and high-capacity delivery systems.

The Acceleration Factor

As companies rush to compress the development cycle, or conception-to-commercialization, speed becomes the competitive edge that enables successful companies to seize control of market opportunities. Acceleration is everything, an especially crucial point in global competition and integral to the factors of productivity and quality. In the late 1980s, Japanese auto makers were still leading the world auto industry in new model introductions, bringing models out every two to three years, versus four to five years for U.S. car makers. By the early 1990s, most of the U.S. carmakers had reduced that gap to almost zero, and made huge strides in quality improvements.

At issue also, however, is our "human" ability to maximize technological alternatives. As the average human life span increases, the generation life span for machines is contracting. There is now a new robotics generation every three to five years, a new computer generation roughly every 18 months, and that span is decreasing. Can we say that the human mind is evolving correspondingly? Or, must we face the fact that our technological capabilities have progressed far beyond people's abilities to master and optimize them? If so, then as we examine the possibilities of our most advanced technologies, our systems must be configured to address the challenges of our biggest bottleneck: How to connect electronic information systems with the human mind.

Communication Speed

One of the reasons we are so aware of the accelerating rate of change is the immediacy of electronic media. Slow-paced linear communication forms like newspapers and books often are being superceded by fast-moving, parallel communications processes ranging from fax machines, telephones, and basic computers, to interactive television, the Internet, and multimedia databases. These bombard our senses with both reliable information and with misinformation and are one of the factors driving pervasive societal changes.

Until the turn of the century, most Americans — except the Indians, who had a highly effective distance communication system using smoke signals — relied on the mails to communicate across geographic distances. Overland mail traveling by stagecoach from Missouri to California took about 25 days. By 1860, the Pony Express had shaved this time to about 10 days, and by 1869 the railroads had reduced letter delivery from Boston to San Francisco to a mere four and a half days. Although the telegraph was in use by the 1850s, it was generally too expensive for the average citizen to use except in an emergency. Despite its expense, however, imagine what a "mutant" communications form the telegraph represented. It was a radically different approach to communications that accelerated human contact from 30 miles per hour to the speed of light.

Setting Time Zones

In a manner that provides an especially appropriate analogy to today's personal computers, the early telegraph was demonstrated by playing chess long-distance. However, the commercial applications quickly followed, and transformed the world in short order. In fact, the combination of the railroads and the adaptation of the telegraph led to the formalization and implementation of time zones in the U.S. in 1883.

Until then, communities and cities were almost autonomous and set their own times according to the position of the sun. The advent of transcontinental railroads and the need for scheduling of trains, along with the abilities of the telegraph to disperse this information, led to adoption of rigorous time zones.[11] The telegraph turned man from a sun-based animal with local orientation to an analog clock-based organism with global orientation.[12]

The telegraph not only increased communications speed and changed man's sense of time, it also gave rise to the great industrial monopoly, Western Union. Western Union, the first electronic communications empire, was the prototype for many of the industrial and communications conglomerates that are part of our global society today.[13]

Michael Angelo Garvey, a writer commenting on the effects of steam and electricity on mankind in 1852, prophesied the future with what seems incredible clarity. He predicted that in some "future period" there would be, "A perfect network of electric filaments" to "consolidate and harmonize the social union of mankind by furnishing a sensitive apparatus analogous to the nervous system of the living frame."[14]

Future Shock in Perspective

While today we ruminate on the societal effects of future shock and new communications technologies, imagine what the sudden appearance of the telegraph represented in future shock to the farmer, the seamstress working at home, the general store manager and all those who had based their daily rhythms wholly on sun time and seasonal changes.

The combination of the telegraph and the railroad finalized the rupture between industrialized and agrarian societies and paved the way for the even more dramatic technological changes that were about to occur. It also provided new definitions for the developed world vs. the undeveloped world. Those concepts gave rise to new schools of economic and political thought and were the basis for distribution of wealth and resources which have held sway for most of the ensuing century.

On March 10, 1876, Alexander Graham Bell and Thomas A. Watson had the world's first phone conversation. Within the next twenty-five years, Americans embraced this new communications technology and by 1915 were using transcontinental telephone service to call San Francisco from New York City. Cables enabled transatlantic phone calls between New York and London by 1927.

Radio technology was refined and commercialized by the mid-twenties, and radio stations were springing up across the country. Radio was the country's first experience with broadcast electronic communications, and Americans loved it. Radio became a very successful conduit of two items in great demand: entertainment and information. Although people still couldn't see the news, they could now hear information about world events, often within hours of their occurrence.

TV as Transforming Technology

Following World War II, television surpassed radio as the transforming technology of the century. Its ability to entertain and reach into living rooms, from Portland, to Pretoria, to Perth, grabbed the imagination of the world. It was a cultural and societal phenomenon. Television was very much a mass media and America was on its way to becoming a mass culture. With the advent of satellite transmission in the late 1960s, events taking place literally a million miles away had immediate impact in our living rooms and on our lives.

Though similar to radio in its timeliness, television had none of the detachment of radio. Its riveting images of all manner of information and events allowed viewers to experience the McCarthy hearings, the Nixon-Kennedy debates, Khruschev's vow to bury America, the Vietnam war, the Apollo moon landing, the Challenger disaster, the dismantling of the Berlin Wall, the fiery night skies of the Gulf War, the Dole, Perot, and Clinton electronic presidential campaigns, the Clinton impeachment hearings, town meetings, and cable television talk shows.

Within two decades of its introduction, television found a place in the home of nearly four in five American families. By the 1970s, television had become the battlefield of choice for America's competing ideological forces. Although special interest groups of all sorts were realizing the power inherent in a mass communications tool, the media "channels," both print and broadcast, were for the most part controlled by the three broadcast networks or by major national publishing companies. The Public Broadcasting System was conceived as an alternative to the sitcoms and soul-numbing violence offered nightly on broadcast television, but even public television became a government subsidized business that was primarily a mass-medium offering, appealing mainly to an affluent audience.

From Mass Media to Individual Voice

Toffler was ahead of his time when he asserted that advancing communications technologies were "quietly and rapidly de-monopolizing communications without a shot being fired," with the result being "a rich de-standardization of cultural output."[15]

Yet, he predicted accurately what has happened in the three decades that have passed since his observation.

Communications technology advances have empowered the individual and the community. What used to be discrete, unrelated communications media are giving way to a rich, seamless mix of integrated technologies that are opening up previously "closed" arenas. For example, broadcast network monopolies have found their turf shrinking under the assault of cable's niche programming, which in turn has lost market share to direct satellite services. Telephone monopolies have at least temporarily lost ground to entrepreneurial alternatives, including Internet long-distance service. Meanwhile, personal computers and the Internet are delivering a vast array of information into the hands of individuals, thus broadening the daily database of information available to the public far beyond the confines of local newspapers. The effects of these changes have been obscured by debates concerning technical standards and censorship. Yet their long-term implications are tremendously important, because at issue is the ability of the individual to *have* access to a diversity of information sources and their enabling technologies.

Communications advances and applications in the last decade of the 20th century have elevated a thousand fold the ability of individuals and interest groups to speak for themselves. True, much of broadcast television and radio is still controlled by a few monolithic companies or by governments. But average citizens are becoming increasingly sophisticated in using communication technologies that allow them to create, produce, and distribute their own messages regarding opinions, research, personal experiences, and philosophy. Tape recorders, fax and photo-copying machines, video cameras and video cassette recorders, cable television's local access studios, cellular phones, on-line personal computers, and the Internet are all technologies that enable the individual not only to create the message, but to control its delivery.

The Cable Generation

This empowerment has extended to television through the diversity offered by cable television, which was responsible for creating a multitude of specialized channels. Cable enabled the breakout from network/national/mass audience control.

The children of the 1950s were our first television generation, raised on the homogeneous offerings of the three broadcast networks. Those who grew up during the '70s and '80s are the first cable television generation, used to a diverse spectrum of specialized programs: MTV, C-SPAN, CNN, Nickelodeon, The Discovery Channel, QVC, Knowledge TV, Black Entertainment Television, The Disney Channel, Galavision, and HBO. All are based on the concept of narrowcasting, or tailored programming that meets the interests of a specific group. It is anticipated that cable will continue to develop in this direction, evolving into even more of an "a la carte" format that will enable subscribers to choose exactly which program they wish to see, when they want to see it. Over time the new major TV broadcast networks will decrease in market power and simply become major cable, direct broadcast satellite (DBS) and perhaps Internet channels.

Based wholly on entreprenuership and risk-taking, cable rarely receives its due credit from media pundits, who tend to lay all television advancements at the feet of the big three U.S. television networks. Cable was, in fact, the technology that broke the TV monopoly and created a medium of abundant options for viewers and opportunities for entrepreneurs. At the same time, cable has been expensive compared to "free" broadcasts of TV, though cable subscribers get more per dollar spent in quality and quantity than from any other information distribution medium. The cable industry has actually been the engine of change for television in the last quarter of the 20th century and is currently morphing into a new array of communications mediums. These converging technologies are bringing TV, radio, the Internet, and telephone delivery together, primarily using digitally-enhanced or digitally-based services.

A significant aspect of specialized cable television services is local origination programming, which allows cable operators and others in local communities to create, produce, and televise those events and issues most important to their fellow citizens. This is an excellent example of Free Market Fusion in action, and was a precursor to Internet-based on-line communities.

The Internet as a Transforming Force

The most obvious and relevant example of the rapid communications proliferation is the Internet. World-wide Internet use was estimated at somewhere around 151 million individuals on-line in December 1998, with a growth rate of 10-20 percent a month.[16]

While the flaws and inadequacies of the Internet are the topic of on-going debate, the "Net" will undoubtedly be known as the leading technological phenomena of the final decade of the 20th century. It has grown from a few thousand regular users in government and academia in the mid-1980s, to a global consumer and commercial communications stream. The Internet is redefining personal communication styles, as well as publishing, financial and business information data gathering, product distribution systems, and telecommunications organizations. And it has created the new phenomena of electronic commerce, which soon will be a multi-trillion dollar industry.[17]

The Internet and its derivatives and successors must be viewed as an entirely new industry. Eventually, it will be even more pervasive than radio and television as we currently experience them. Indeed, many existing technologies will be largely morphed into the Internet, and Internet technology will be fused ever more deeply into processes like education, healthcare and government. In so doing, the Internet delivers more power and opportunity into the hands of the entrepreneurs.

The North American Internet, global in its reach, is a potential blueprint for regional Internets in Asia and elsewhere. (The Asia Internet will be the subject of a case study available at *freemarketfusion.com* at a later date).

In the coming decade, grass roots organizations, using cable, satellite and the Internet, will have the opportunity to gain in power and visibility through increased and more effective use of state-of-the-art communications tools. These are technologies of freedom, and they can transfer power from governments, other institutions, and even businesses to individuals. Organized, empowered citizens already are demanding the right to participate not just in the discussions, but in the decisions.

Electronic democracy already has changed the way developed democracies govern themselves. Internationally, as telecommunications advances continue to dismantle national information borders, people will increasingly have the chance to realize that they *all* may want peace, regardless of what their governments are telling them. This harkens back to President Eisenhower's post-war remark that "people want peace so much that one of these days governments had better get out of the way and let them have it."

That's the good news about technology evolution and its benefits. But accompanying this upward spiral of choice and cheaper technology is a colossal struggle for control of the access pipes and what in the way of entertainment, information, and even political "spin" flows through them.

The great opportunity presented here is the opportunity to provide an arena of explosive business growth if the Internet and all telecommunications bandwidth does not become controlled by a monopoly or fettered by government regulation.

If these two major pitfalls are avoided, the horizon for Free Market Fusion that embraces the Internet and its successors will be bright indeed.

An Interview with Alvin and Heidi Toffler: Three Decades of "Future Shock"

The Tofflers are authors of *Future Shock*, *The Third Wave*, *Powershift*, *War and Anti-War*, and five other books on global change.

Have you changed your premise, first stated in your book *Future Shock*, published in 1970, about the increasing acceleration of change and its chaotic effects on modern society?

Tofflers: No. We have not changed that basic assumption. In the late 1960s we researched and wrote *Future Shock*. When we told people we were writing about the acceleration of change, the typical response was, "What is that?"

And why do people react more positively to your ideas today?

Today there is no question in people's minds that life is moving very rapidly. That it's difficult to keep pace with changes in the workplace, in society, and technology, and in almost every aspect of life. Acceleration pressures are a fact of life.

What hasn't turned out the way you expected?

Tofflers: There were some minor points that we made that didn't materialize. For example, there was a chapter on throw-away things, and one of the examples that we talked about was paper clothing. That never did catch on. But that was essentially a trivial example of a larger, more fundamental point that was correct: We're now seeing a faster through-put of things in our lives, people in our lives, ideas and information in our lives, organizational structures in our lives, and so on. So, we think the overall point was correct. But there were some examples that did not materialize as we had expected.

Were there any major things you would change?

Tofflers: The central weakness of what we said in *Future Shock* twenty-nine years ago was the assumption that the economy was essentially going to continue to grow, without major ups and downs. At the time, we were young and naive and accepted uncritically what the economists were saying at the time. Economists claimed they knew how to manage an economy so well that all we had to do was "fine tune it" and that would prevent any significant recessions or upheavals. As it turned out, *Future Shock*, which was accused of being a radical book, was insufficiently radical.

How could you have been more radical at the time?

Tofflers: Had we followed our own thesis all the way, it would have been plain to us that you could not have the kinds of changes we were talking about in technology and a dozen other fields without also having significant changes in the economy. The idea that the economy would just continue to grow in a linear fashion without ups and downs was a trend projection which was common among economists at the time, and which was in fact dead wrong. We have since been leery not only of economists, but of trend projection.

Those beliefs are eerily similar to some of the things we were hearing about "the economy that can't be stopped."

Tofflers: Yes. There are two schools of thought about prosperity in America. One side is traditionalist. It holds that the stock market is way overblown and the old fundamentals of the economy remain unchanged. Therefore, the values attributed to various companies today by the stock market are completely unrealistic and we are doomed to a stock market crash.

The counter-argument holds that there is a "new economy" which in fact is seldom described very adequately but in very rough terms parallels our description of what a third wave economy might be like. What's wrong with both these positions is their simplicity. We believe that there is, in fact, a new economy, but that does not mean that it is going to be a stable economy or that we're going to enjoy twenty-five years of boom times as some futurists have forecast. It seems to us there's no contradiction in saying we are in fact dealing with a dramatically new kind of economy, but that the economy has certain risks of instability and non-equilibrium conditions. Some economists are finally beginning to take seriously the increasing importance of intangible capital and various other ideas about which we have written for decades. One who is doing some fresh and extremely valuable work is Paul Romer at Stanford.

In an interview in *Wired* magazine a few years ago, you referred to the possibility that certain types of information might be "blocked," or censored, in the future. Were you referring to information on cloning, for example?

Tofflers: One of the fundamental philosophical/ political issues that's going to confront us in the years ahead has precisely to do with the question: Is there knowledge that we should not pursue? It has been the ethic of science for the past three centuries that we should be free to pursue knowledge in any direction. This is, in fact, a very important value, not only in the United States, but throughout the Western world. We believe that the moral issues that will confront us as a result of the genetics revolution — issues having to do with the potentials for Nazi-style eugenics, for example — will lead to a questioning of this ethic, and that therefore we will hear more and more demands and cries to cut off research or thinking in certain fields.

How would you characterize Joe and Jane Sixpack, your hypothetical typical American family in *Future Shock*, today?

Tofflers: One of the main themes of our work has focused on the increasing internal differentiation of society, the growing diversity that is made possible by the "third wave" [The Tofflers' second book is *The Third Wave*, which describes the information-driven society].

If we are correct that in fact we are moving toward a more highly diversified and more individualized society, with customized products, information flows and banking services, then it stands to reason that we also will see greater diversity in family forms. That old industrial age slogan, "one size fits all," will be replaced in every field by "one size misfits all." And we believe that goes for family structure as well. This does not necessarily mean that people don't want family or that they don't want children or that they don't seek companionship and love and that they don't have responsibility toward each other. It does mean, however, that the old family definition of the house with the white picket fence, the husband who goes to work, the wife who stays home with two children under the age of eighteen, is not the right model for everybody. We believe we will see relentless advances in the understanding by society that multiple family forms do not represent the death of a family, but rather the development of the family system to a higher level of complexity.

What do you see as the primary challenges of the new economy to the U.S. k-12 public education system?

Tofflers: We have, at present, a factory-style mass education system that was perfectly geared for turning out people to either work in factories or live in societies dominated by factory principles. And the result is that we're preparing — in the United States particularly — millions upon millions of young people for jobs and ways of life that are quite unlikely to be there when they become adults. We are spending probably half a trillion dollars a year on a mass education machine. And most proposals for so-called "education reform" are essentially aimed at making the machine run more efficiently rather than getting rid of the machine and truly moving toward more individualized education. Children are treated as raw material entering into a factory. They're processed and inspected going in. They're made to do rote and repetitive work and to show up obediently and punctually, and then they're inspected at the end of the line. Then they are ready to go to work in an environment which requires rote and repetitive work, punctuality, and obedience. This rust-belt system is almost beyond repair.

How would you characterize the U.S. higher education system?

We think there's a significant difference between the high school factory and the university, which clearly offers a greater diversity. And in general does a better job.

In your books you have referred frequently to the rise of conflicts among economic groups, such as agrarian vs. industrial vs. information-based groups. Most new businesses and ventures today require a keen sensitivity to global issues and conflicts because they directly impact economics and markets. What rule of thumb would you offer to a new international business venture?

Tofflers: We don't believe we can reduce everything to a simple formula. But in general, if we look back at history, we can see quite clearly that whenever the second wave or industrial revolution arrived, it was immediately followed by conflict between the innovators and so-called "modernists," versus the old "elites" that dominated the previous agrarian society. We call that "first wave, second wave conflict." And if you look around the world today, we believe you can still see it. It's no accident that the former mayor of Belgrade said of the war around Sarajevo some years ago that it was a war of the mountains against the cities. Or the mountain people against the city people. And we believe if you look at many conflicts, you will find that at their heart, they're conflicts between rural people and urban people. The Taliban in Afghanistan came out of the villages and tried to impose the mores the villagers grew up with on an urbanized population in Kabul. If you look at South Africa, for years there was conflict between the African National Congress of Mandela with its large urban base and the Inkatha Freedom Party made up of the more rural Zulus led by Mangosuthu Gatsha Buthelezi. First and second wave conflicts, we believe, are present in many parts of the world, although they are frequently attributed to ethnic, racial, religious or other causes. There's no one single cause for a war or conflict. They frequently have multiple causes. But the collision of different civilizations based on the different waves of change is in fact the master conflict from which most others derive.

You have been somewhat critical of the theories put forth by Samuel Huntington, who wrote a book titled, *The Clash of Civilizations and the Remaking of World Order* (1996), which is used in many university political science courses. Where do you differ?

Tofflers: In our book, *War and Anti-War* (1993), we have a chapter entitled, "The Clash of Civilizations." And shortly after that was published, Samuel Huntington wrote a very influential article for *Foreign Affairs* in which he used the same term, "The Clash of Civilizations."

But our use of the term "civilization" is quite different from Huntington's, which is essentially based on religion. As he sees it, there's an Islamic civilization, a Confucian civilization, a Hindu civilization, a Judeo-Christian civilization, and so forth. We believe that Huntington's image of these civilizations is exceedingly static. He sees these civilizations as essentially unchanging. With the decline of ideological conflict between communism and capitalism, he sees the conflict between these essentially immutable civilizations as being the dominant one in the future.

We think that's wrong because every one of these "civilizations" is itself undergoing fundamental change today. The words they use might be the same, but the lives of the people are not necessarily the same and the meanings that they attach to things are not necessarily the same. We think that his is a static, rather Newtonian view of the world. We believe his ultimate conclusion — that we're going to wind up in a world in which it is, as we think he put it, the West against the rest — is a dangerously oversimplified formula. It contributes, at a minimum, to misunderstanding among different cultures and peoples.

We do not identify civilizations with individual religions. Rather, we regard different socio-economic formations (which may include people of different religions) as more decisive. The Neolithic revolution gave rise to a way of life around the world based on village life, human and animal muscle power, and peasant labor regulated by the seasons — an agrarian civilization that has fundamental similarities in different parts of the world, despite religious and cultural differences. The industrial revolution spread an urban industrial civilization that has Judeo-Christian, Confucian, and Shinto-Buddhist variations.

Now a new civilization is beginning to emerge, built around knowledge-based economics. Hindu programmers in Bangalore and Confucian programmers in Taiwan might have more in common with each other and Silicon Valley than with their co-religionists. And new religions are arising. We think the splits between peasant civilization and the new, emergent civilization will be more decisive than Huntington's grouping.

In this social-political environment, do you have any recommendations for entrepreneurs in the 21st century, as to where they should look for opportunities?

Tofflers: You, Glenn Jones, have said that the three big fields of the future are going to be health, education and environment, and that there are ways to make enormous fortunes and do good in each of these fields. And we believe that's undoubtedly correct. We would, of course, add that there are enormous opportunities opening up not just in biotechnology, for example, or in electronics, but in the services. We are an under-serviced society. The emphasis on manufacturing has been so intense during the industrial era, that there are myriad forms of service that simply don't exist that would help improve our lives, make us more comfortable, make us healthier, safer and happier. We believe we're going to see an explosion of niche services in society and that these will make use of networks and computers and telecommunications. These tools will be there to serve, to support the services. One does not have to be in the network or computer or telecom business in order to find a powerful entrepreneurial niche.

CHAPTER 3

WHAT CHANGE MEANS
How change dominates business

To effectively adapt Free Market Fusion as an entrepreneurial approach, those using it must have reached an accommodation in their professional and personal lives with the reality of rapid change.

What change means, like much else in life, is in the eye of the beholder. To the individual — or institution — invested in the status quo, change inevitably means loss. To government it means loss as power flows to individual citizens. To those — especially entrepreneurs — determined to accept and embrace change as the only immutable in life, change offers opportunity. Opportunity to find new solutions, to try new alternatives, to chart a new, perhaps more effective or humanizing course, and to reap new rewards.

We cannot control change, we can only control our attitudes *about* change. For those of us who embrace the opportunities it offers, change becomes a "new dimension" resource in much the same way that its corollaries, time, distance, and information, have become strategic resources. Managing our attitudes about change is dependent on knowledge. Assembling true knowledge — as opposed to information — allows us to cope with the forces of change and anxiety. Without the knowledge, we encounter the situation described by Richard Saul Wurman in his 1989 book, *Information Anxiety*:

"Information anxiety is produced by the ever-widening gap between what we understand and what we think we should understand. It is the black hole between data and knowledge, and it happens when information doesn't tell us what we want or need to know."[18] (see interview, page 71)

An ideal example of an institution coping with tremendous change is the Library of Congress. Though the unaware passerby might presume that this 200-year-old archive would be a bastion of resistance to new technology and trends, it is in fact a leader in implementing new information tools and access pathways.

If other government officials can follow the Library's example, they could play a pivotal role in helping the entrepreneurial guidance of change.

Powershift and World Leadership

Things have been different for the generation of adults now on center stage in the business, political, and cultural arenas. These leaders came of age and had their assumptions shaped between 1965 and 1985, an era when change was the norm and stability a fleeting and not-to-be-trusted aberration.

This group includes U.S. President Bill Clinton, former U.S. House of Representatives Speaker Newt Gingrich, Mexico President Ernesto Zadillo, Czech Republic head of state Vaclav Havel, Ireland's President Mary McAleese and Peru's President Alberto Fujimori. This group also includes many of the top staff and advisors of Russian President Boris Yeltsen and many of the Western-educated officials and advisors within the People's Republic of China's top echelon. All fall into the "powershift" generation. The term applies to those who ride the wave of constant change and regard it as normal.[19]

For the first "TV generation," unremitting change was accepted as simply a key factor of the operating environment. Rather than avoiding change or attempting to control the rate of its advance, many of today's adults have chosen to thrive on change, and to seek it out. For these individuals, stability equates with a stifling stagnation. This response is even stronger for the present generation of youth, the "video game generation," which has been raised in an environment of instantaneous, parallel electronic communication.

Is this casual acceptance of change a detriment or a benefit?

I believe it is the latter, especially since history teaches us that the ability to respond rapidly and easily to change proves in the long run to be a highly effective adaptive skill, ensuring the survival of a species in a changing environment. None of the non-human living organisms inhabiting the earth have ever been able to nullify change or the rate at which it occurs. Instead, all have had but one compelling fate: Adapt or die.

Given the stark simplicity of these options, it becomes evident that we must determine not how to control the rate of change, but how to identify and teach the skills necessary to excel in an environment of pervasive, incessant change.

The most important of these skills is attitude. Our attitudes frame our responses to stimulus. If we accept that change represents opportunity rather than threat, then we can see in its outcomes growth rather than destabilization, diversity rather than fragmentation, and freedom rather than fear.

Change Resistors

History gives us examples of species, civilizations, and, more recently, commercial enterprises that were unable or unwilling to adapt to change. The wooly mammoth, the Roman Empire and Digital Equipment Corp. all represent this phenomena.

Darwin's survival of the fittest theory was, in essence, survival of the most adaptable. History demonstrates that it has been no different for individuals and nations, companies and conglomerates.

Many eastern European governments once were identified as change resistors because of their Communist systems. Their abilities to embrace change — cultural, political, and economic — are more widely recognized now, as they have adapted to new freedoms. Russia, meanwhile, has become mired in a no-give tug of war between those who want change, and its traditional power groups that resist it.

China has taken a different route to change, one that embraces Communism while seeking to adopt capitalistic market techniques, and perhaps new models are evolving. But the ways in which these countries seek to apply the lessons of Western-brand capitalism involve more than a little uncertainty.

Business history offers a wealth of examples of the sorry demise of modern-day dinosaurs, those organizations unable, unwilling, or too slow to adapt to change. In most cases, a more enlightened management approach could have produced early examples of Free Market Fusion.

The railroads probably hold the dubious honor of being the most frequently cited example of poor business judgment and a total inability to understand and respond to changing market environment. Mistakenly believing themselves to be in the "railroad business," the business of moving freight and passengers by rail, the 19th century railroad magnates' empires disintegrated as the 20th century brought an array of competing transportation "and communication business" alternatives. Had they been able to broaden their vision to see the transportation and communications business as their arena, quite possibly they could have created, adapted and exploited these new technologies themselves (see Jay Gould, page 60).

Encyclopedia Britannica, the dominant force in home libraries for decades, ignored the trend toward on-line and CD-ROM information publishing, until competitors had whittled away significant portions of its market share.

Similar stories abound. In fact, any company, depending on attitude and flexibility, is at risk of dinosaur syndrome. By refusing to acknowledge the changing market environment brought on by higher gas prices, smaller families, and younger, more style-conscious consumers, in the 1970s the American automobile industry lost a crippling percentage of its customer base to small, sporty, gas-efficient imports. Then, in an even more crippling misreading of customers, companies like General Motors for decades apparently failed to understand the difference between marketing quality that did not really exist in their products of that era and actually creating quality.

The U.S. Postal Service is another case in point. Remaining essentially unchanged since its original charter in 1789, the U.S. government's mail service has virtually given away major portions of its market to companies using technology to deliver messages, packages, and data faster, cheaper, and more reliably. Finally returned to profitability in the mid-1990s after several years of difficult, chaotic change, the USPS continues to operate as a monopoly in major portions of its market and still has a considerable debt burden to payoff.

Ma Bell's Missed Opportunity

U.S. telephone companies (the original AT&T of "ma bell and the baby bells") are another example of industry leaders with a history of resisting, rather than leading, change. Funding research in electronic communications, but failing to implement the results, U.S. telephone companies led the way in electronics advances (including the development of the coaxial cable ultimately used by entrepreneurial cable television companies) but then never bothered to timely deploy them to improve, expand, or reduce the cost of basic telephone service.

Essentially monopolies, the phone companies had no reason to upgrade their product until forced into a competitive environment when they were dismantled in 1984. By then, cable television companies already had effectively maximized the potential of coaxial cables, as they are now maximizing the potential of fiber optic lines to the home.

Despite their best efforts, the phone companies were unable to control the speed of change. They were no longer able to control the schedule on which new technology inserted itself into the market. They failed to comprehend that the speed of change itself had become a driving factor, no longer controllable. In this case, change meant that the telephone companies lost a new opportunity by their blind adherence to old (and not-yet depreciated) solutions. They temporarily lost their position of utter dominance.

The baby bells have now gone into fiber, though their old attitudes regarding exclusive markets and price models tend to prevail. This situation keeps the door of opportunity open for cable companies and others to move into the telephone and data transmission markets.

Because change resistors in the long run are unable to stop the forward progress of change, they simply enable others to embrace the opportunities they have chosen to ignore.

Clearly, AT&T's new CEO Michael Armstrong "gets it," but it will be interesting to see if the AT&T culture and bureaucracy will learn the lesson missed by its progeny. Moving into cable and beginning to reconstitute itself through its acquisition of TCI and others, AT&T now has a considerable opportunity. We will see if it listens to the entrepreneurial advice of its acquired companies and the people who run them, such as TCI CEO John Malone and that company's president, the indefatigable Leo Hindry.

Mavericks of Change

For every enterprise that has failed to understand and seize the opportunities inherent in change, others have risen eagerly and successfully to the challenge.

Jay Gould founded Western Union, an electronic communications business, by stringing wire along the railroad rights-of-way. Present day railroad magnate and world-class entrepreneur Philip Anschutz has emulated Gould's model by successfully using his railroad rights-of-way to lay fiber optic cable for his new Qwest long distance telephone company.

Another example is entrepreneur and presidential candidate Ross Perot, who founded his data processing firm, Electronic Data Systems (EDS), in the mid-1960s.

An Annapolis graduate who joined IBM immediately upon discharge from military service, Perot was attracted to the corporate culture, including the ardent customer service and personal ethic requirements of the world's largest computer company. Even so, Perot claims that he spotted huge gaps in the customer service areas of IBMs practice, and he quickly set up his own firm to begin tailoring software.

Perot refined his approach after leaving IBM and while working for the Dallas office of Blue Cross (one of IBM's biggest customers) for five years.[20] He was forced to resign from Blue Cross when company officials became suspicious that he was using his position to design a strategy to start his own consulting business with Blue Cross as a client. Still, Perot's new company was a success, thanks largely to the fact that he had designed software to meet Blue Cross needs. This was something IBM had failed to provide, and which other Blue Cross managers apparently would not demand from their computer supplier. Perot used the same formula for service with other IBM customers, including the U.S. government and General Motors. GM eventually bought EDS from Perot for an exorbitant price.

Apple Computer: The Mouse that Roared

In the early 1980s, about the same time that Perot was being courted by GM,[21] IBM was under another assault .

Apple Computer's Steve Jobs and his partner Steven Wozniak rewrote business history when, in a combination of extraordinary, passionate vision and awesome naiveté, they believed that their garage-based computer company could go head-to-head with IBM in a market it dominated. Yet they understood two key changes in the computer market that IBM, focused on its corporate customers, failed to exploit.

First, computer technology had advanced to such an extent that computers could now be downsized and produced inexpensively enough to serve the individual, not just businesses. Second, as computers and an understanding of their capabilities had become commonplace in offices, more and more people were visualizing personal uses for their computers. But the computers had to be smaller, portable, less expensive, and — most importantly — easier to use.

IBM gave little credence to these changes in its environment. So Jobs and Wozniak grabbed the ball, developed the people's computer, and placed it in the hands of students and teachers throughout the country. Apple then moved into big successes in the multi-media and desktop publishing and graphic design markets.

The company continued to score touchdowns through the 1970s and 1980s. But it began to suffer its own "change resistor" syndrome in the 1990s, as the company's management became formalized and proved unable to adapt quickly to new market trends, the same affliction for which Apple's founders had consistently criticized IBM and turned into its initial market opportunity a few years earlier. After enormous fiscal losses, several unsuccessful attempts at being acquired and a rapid succession of top management changes, the company returned to profitability under Job's leadership in 1998, but still faces an uncertain future.

Cable's Great Leap Forward

When the U.S.'s first cable line was hooked up[22] in the late 1940s, cable television was simply a means to improve reception for the nation's three networks. However, by the early 1970s, it had become evident to cable entrepreneur Chuck Dolan that although there were essentially only three choices for television programs, there was a nearly inexhaustible appetite among Americans for entertainment.

Although the networks responded to this demand by ignoring it, Dolan seized the opportunity. In 1972, with the financial backing of Time, Inc., he launched the Home Box Office (HBO) service, telecasting *Sometimes a Great Notion* to 325 customers in Wilkes-Barre, Pennsylvania.[23]

Three years later, Gerry Levin, then-president of Home Box Office, received approval from the FCC to use communications satellites to send HBO programs into cable-wired homes throughout the country.

Satellites provided national distribution, replacing microwave transmission's unreliability. Seeing the opportunity and moving rapidly to exploit it for HBO's subscribers, Levin positioned HBO to become one of the leading national entertainment networks. In 1998, HBO had 26.7 million subscribers.[24] Industry analysts estimate its revenues to be well in excess of $1.5 billion. Based on that visionary leap, by mid-1998 cable television — and an abundance of program choices largely created by entrepreneurs — had become a part of 66 percent of America's homes, or 65.1 million households.[25]

Change continued to offer opportunities to entrepreneurs who would seize them. As its appetite for entertainment was expanding, so was America's appetite for information. The change taking place, an increased market for news and related programming, offered a tremendous challenge and a tremendous reward to anyone who would take it on. Although the networks' response to this opportunity was confined to fine-tuning their existing news programs — essentially repeating the formats they had used for more than three decades — entrepreneur Ted Turner envisioned and created an entirely new product: a 24-hour news channel. And it was based in Atlanta, not the world-media-center, New York City, which elicited hoots of derision from network executives in their Manhattan offices.

Since its inception in 1980, Turner's brainchild, the Cable News Network (CNN), has continued to break ground with its gutsy, pioneering news reporting. Incredibly successful by all measures, Turner's 24-hour news channel is now feeling the effects of that highest form of flattery, with new competitors trying to imitate CNN and with the 1996 friendly acquisition by Time Warner.

The entrepreneurs of the computer industry — Jobs, Gates, Moore, Grove and others — demonstrated similar maverick insights. TCI head John Malone, the chief architect of the cable industry as we know it today, consistently displays similar insights. Most recently his focus on TV and computer convergence via set-top box research and development, plus his careful direction of TCI's strategic alliance with computer industry entrepreneurs, has given new strength to the cable industry's competition with conventional broadcasting.

Clearly, many of the heroes of the communications revolution initially have been those outsiders who were able to perceive and pursue possibilities where industry insiders saw only obstacles. Their vision was derided by the vested interests they bested, but those heroes understood that change was not only inevitable, it was opportunity in its purest and most exhilarating form. By persevering, they created a new future, a future that is still evolving explosively.

Dissolving Boundaries and New Ideas

Perhaps the most important symptom of change in the closing decade of the 20th century has been the dissolving of boundaries we have taken for granted for centuries. Although the world is focused today on the national boundaries that, in an information-flow context, are dissolving all around us, the boundaries that delineate distinct ideas and activities also are giving way. These boundaries have served to separate such concepts as learning versus playing, education versus employment, home versus office, and industry versus industry. The lines defining these relationships, once clearly drawn, are now blurring in the shadow of convergence. Embedded in all these areas of convergence are potential opportunities for Free Market Fusion initiatives.

Although philosophically the concept of "seamless living" has always been a given, today it is also becoming a lifestyle reality. Consider the transitional movements now underway:

Learning/playing. Albert Einstein said, "Imagination is more important than knowledge." That might well be the motto for many excellent early childhood TV learning programs. Innovative educational technologies enable us to integrate games and play into highly effective learning situations by building on our children's natural propensities and curiosities. The innovative programming developed for "Sesame Street" by The Children's Television Workshop (CTW) is an early example of crossing the learning/playing boundary. The model and basic concept developed and demonstrated by CTW proved so effective that it has now been integrated not only into innovative television programs, but also into interactive and computer-based activities.

Education/employment. Companies and their employees are now recognizing that lifelong education and skills enhancement are critical to an increased level of American productivity and competitiveness. According to the American Society of Training and Development, U.S. companies spend in excess of $30 billion annually to upgrade their employees' skills or retrain them for other jobs. Much of this training takes place on-site at the corporate facilities, rather than on college campuses. In fact, many companies — among them Hewlett Packard, IBM, United Airlines, Xerox, Ford and General Motors — have set up their own "corporate classrooms." IBM, with an annual education budget of more than $1 billion, runs an educational system that surpasses the expenditures of even the largest cities' public school systems.

Home/office. Many information-based jobs no longer have to be performed at the corporate site. Although not yet commonplace, telecommuters now make up a substantial portion of the American work force. Additionally, home-based businesses are springing up as the solution of choice for more and more American parents trying to combine professional and parental commitments. The benefits to all parties involved in telecommuting are substantial. They include more productive use of time for the employee (no commute, no mornings spent "getting ready" for work, no interruptions from associates), more effective allocation of office space for the employer, and, for the community, a reduction in the amount of automobile pollution spewing out each day.

A similar boundary that has fallen for many U.S. families is that between home and school. According to the U.S. Department of Education, between 250,000 and 350,000 children are now being taught by parents who have chosen home schooling as an alternative to public education.[26] Believing that their ability to educate their children surpasses that of public-school teachers, these parents have chosen to create an education environment within their homes.

Industry/industry. Whereas most businesses once were able to clearly define what business and which industry they were in, today many of us find that the businesses and industries in which we started out no longer have neatly defined borders. In fact, during these chaotic times, envisioning and going after opportunities well beyond our traditional business borders is the only strategy that will allow companies to survive, let alone flourish.

The cable television industry provides an excellent example of this trend. What was once a group of companies organized to enhance and deliver broadcast television signals to geographically remote locations is now an industry that incorporates technologies drawn from the telephone, computer, and communications industries, as well as concepts, products, services and expertise drawn from the entertainment/programming, information, and education industries. The broadband digital network — merging audio, video, and data through digitization — increasingly will blur the lines between telephony, cable, and computers. It also will powerfully impact existing product distribution systems, especially if the products actually can be digitized. The new wireless telephone technologies — fiber optic lines, and digital signal compression — are combining to drive the development of a myriad of innovative cable/telephone/computer-based products and services.

Cable television companies move into developing phone networks, telephone companies continue to pursue joint strategies leading to the delivery of video, and computer companies explore the opportunities inherent in the evolving distribution technologies. And all of them try to break the economic code of the Internet.

Is change a threat or an opportunity for Free Market Fusion processes? Although no answers are set in stone, there is one certainty: boundaries will only damage those who continue to cling to them.

In fact, vast new horizons will open up continually for those strategically savvy companies willing to leave behind their old precepts and platforms, and to fully explore the emerging technologies. This may mean casting off a process or technology that was "new" only months before. But for Free Market Fusion enterprises, an environment of constant change provides the critical foundation for constant opportunity.

An Interview with
Richard Saul Wurman

Wurman is author of *Information Anxiety* and *Follow the Yellow Brick Road*, creator of Access books and TED (the Technology, Entertainment and Design conference).

What is the difference between information inundation and information glut?

Wurman: I believe there is a glut of data, and that too much is written in a form that is just not understandable. When things are of interest and understandable, then there isn't too much. A good example is the child who has trouble learning math in school, but readily understands and computes baseball batting and pitching statistics. If it's relevant to their interests, they get it very quickly.

Is there a level of anxiety dysfunction which some form of information access can remedy? Is your bottom line advice to anyone, simply, "Don't be afraid to ask?"

Wurman: It's a little more complex than that. Learning is based on pattern recognition, recognizing something familiar. We learn in school that an acre has 43,560 square feet, but that statistic doesn't create an image in our minds, and most of us forget it very quickly. But, for an American at least, if you know that an acre is about the size of a football field without the end zones, you'll probably remember it the rest of your life. So, if you can attach something familiar to data, sort of like putting velcro on the ends and sticking it to something, there's a better chance of coping with information anxiety.

Why has information come to be commonly misconstrued as knowledge?

Wurman: Data isn't information and information doesn't become knowledge without the individual having an interest in it and needing to apply it. The misunderstanding of the differences is just sloppiness in how we talk about these terms in our culture.

What one best tool do you recommend be employed for judicious selection of information?

Wurman: Again, it's interest. You have to embrace your own interests and realize that a good question is better than a brilliant answer. We don't teach courses in how to ask a good question, or how to have a good conversation, or in how to organize information. There are five basic ways of organizing information, one which is man-made — alphabetization — and we give over the first five years of schooling to learning it. The other four aren't formally taught, but also work very well, and they are location, time, category, and hierarchy. Each kind of information tells you how it wants to be organized, and once you can retrieve the information, then you have your best tool.

What is an example of an ideal information template, a favorite of yours?

Wurman: One of my favorites is the show, "Franklin and Jefferson," by Charles Eames. The main key was to organize the critical events of these two famous men's lives in two parallel time lines, because they lived some of their lives at the same time and they crossed over in many of the things that they did. That is a fascinating way to arrange an exhibition about their lives and that era, by the time lines of their two lives.

Would you comment on disposable information — that which becomes obsolete in hours or days — versus keystone information or transcendent information that retains its worth, and how to assign value or bench mark each type?

Wurman: Disposable information is valuable, but it's like playing gin rummy. If you're a good card player, you remember everything about the cards while you're playing that hand, and forget it the second the hand is over because you don't need it anymore. But you always remember the rules of gin rummy, which is transcendent information. Transcendent information is important to us, and we learn it and remember it for that reason. We associate it with, or attach it to things that are important to us. There shouldn't be guilt associated with either type, just an importance in remembering either type for as long as we need it.

Much of contemporary management practice presumes that future planning or posturing has little to do with operational reality and planning in "real world" information settings. Would you comment on how to convert a scenario, or strategic planning outcome, into an effective set of future-oriented instructions?

Wurman: The problem with future planning is a cultural problem. In most companies, people want something to deposit in the bank by tomorrow afternoon. Once, I was at a company and asked what was the key motivation of the top manager I was about to meet. I was told, "Retirement." Recognition and embracing of our own mortality can lead to terribly wrong decisions in the corporate world. To get management or stockholders to assign importance to long range planning and what it may point to, you have to figure out how to assign value to it. In some industries or companies, this just may not be possible. Quality often sells, but not always, as the example of Beta video technology losing out to VHS video demonstrates. In the movie industry, quality always sells if you put it in terms of what movie goers like. But the movie producers don't know for sure what the future holds for their endeavor until it's been in the theaters for 10 days.

If a person can convey value and quality through their passion for an idea or product, they may be able to influence those who decide. I begin every day with two guiding thoughts: one, if you don't ask, you don't get; and, two, most things don't work.

CHAPTER 4

COPING WITH CHANGE
How government and education react

In Thomas Jefferson's first inaugural address, delivered March 4, 1801, he described a good government as one that "shall restrain men from injuring one another, which shall leave them otherwise free to regulate their own pursuits of industry and improvement, and shall not take from the mouth of labor the bread it has earned."

As mentioned later in this book, Jefferson also was a leader in the movement toward literacy and education for the general public, in the interest of developing an informed electorate. In the nearly two hundred years since our second president uttered those words, the purview of government has expanded to such a degree that it would be unrecognizable by Jefferson were he to address the nation today.

Perhaps the morphing of technologies will enable the reversal of power flowing to big governments and instead move power from governments and institutions to individuals. Likewise, the public education system Jefferson envisioned is now struggling with such new paradigms as knowledge workers, demands for life-long learning, and professionals who probably will retrain for new careers five to seven times in the course of their 30-year work span.

Jefferson's quote about the necessity of change in government could also be applied to the importance of reform in education:

> "We might as well require a man to wear still the coat which fitted him when a boy as civilized society to remain even under the regimen of their barbarous ancestors."

Both government and the U.S. education system face considerable challenges to begin delivering the services that the citizenry expects.

Government as Impediment

Over the past two centuries Americans have moved from the hands-off approach of government envisioned by the country's founders to government as a principal driver, deliverer, and regulator of American hopes and aspirations. We have ended up with a government unable to offer visionary leadership because it has become so mired in micro-managing. On the other hand, government that responds to instant voter polls may also end up abdicating its basic responsibilities.

However, a slow but certain shifting of priorities seems to be underway among the most innovative government and business leaders. This shift involves a different way of looking at what we want the ultimate responsibility of government to be: should government be the provider of all things to all people, an impossible and appallingly expensive undertaking, as we and others have discovered? Or, should government set the priorities and then let the free enterprise system provide the means and ends, an approach which, though quite imperfect, has served our economy well?

Many communities and their governments are opting for the latter. A number of municipalities are embracing the trend toward privatization, hiring non-governmental companies to provide such services as garbage pickup, environmental recycling, and parks and recreation management.

In effect, private businesses are providing community-mandated government services, usually at a substantial cost savings and with greater efficiency. In fact, more and more state and municipal governments are taking their cue from business strategists and looking at how services are provided in order to maximize the community's return on investment, i.e., tax dollars.

"Entrepreneurial government," an approach advocated by David Osborne and Ted Gaebler in their book *Reinventing Government: How the Entrepreneurial Spirit is Transforming the Public Sector* (1992), is the exact opposite of the cumbersome, sluggish, centralized bureaucratic government under which so much of this country and its economy are currently groaning. This strategy, put forth in further detail in *Banishing Bureaucracy: The Five Strategies for Reinventing Government* (1997), by David Osborne and Peter Plasterik, is also an excellent template for Free Market Fusion. Under this formula, entrepreneurial governments emulate (and occasionally joint-venture with) their private-industry counterparts, engaging in such activities as "investing venture capital, creating private financial institutions, using volunteers to run parks and libraries, swapping real estate, even structuring the market to encourage energy conservation, recycling, and environmental protection."[27]

There is a question whether government truly can be entrepreneurial without the big motivators of a "brass ring" for success and the "deep six" for failure. Regardless, entrepreneurial approaches offer opportunities for private enterprise to contribute and benefit, and also benefit the community, taxpayers, and the local economy.

Another example of business-government crossover is in the area of public schools. There is a predictable and powerful effort on the part of vested public education interests to engage in the rhetoric of change, while simultaneously insuring that serious public funding is denied to private-side initiatives that would force real change. To expect those controlling public education to resolve long standing, and, in many instances, worsening problems, without the insertion of competition and accountability from the private side, is probably unrealistic. (see "Scenarios for Public Education," Appendix B)

To date, private enterprise involvement in this arena includes direct funding, contribution of materials, lending of executives' time and expertise, development of working models for cyber classes, participation in the design of innovative reform efforts such as vouchers, needs-assessment partnerships, and student internship programs, as well as the contracting out of school management directly to private enterprise companies. And this trend is becoming international. For these companies and organizations, there has been a belief that "impossible" was simply a temporary adjective. In an environment of rapid change, yesterday's impossibility is today's opportunity, soon to be tomorrow's historical footnote.

Global Aspects of Change

Information disregards boundaries, including those of repressive governments.

If the human instinct toward freedom is not enough to fuel the long march toward more democratic societies, the realities of competing in the information-driven, knowledge-based, intensely competitive 21st century global marketplace will likely turn the tide.

In fact, this knowledge dynamic has led some economists to propose a new theory of economic growth that adds knowledge into the mix of key factors along with land, labor, and capital. Assigning knowledge a value on a par with, for example, new assembly line equipment, is key to understanding why economies like the U.S. continue to grow and prosper even as their industrial output is shifted to overseas competitors. Growth of technology and technology adaptation are the keys, according to Paul Romer, a professor of economics at Stanford University, who is the champion of the new growth theory.

While the theory can apply to older industries now using "smart" industrial machines that depend on software, Romer and his supporters most readily point to computer, software and biotechnology companies as the best examples of their new economic model. One of the model's fundamentals is that knowledge products have almost all of the costs built into the development of the first unit. Distributing floppy discs with new software to millions of customers gets cheaper and cheaper, and may even cost nothing when done over the Internet. This makes it possible for a producer to eventually make a several thousand percent profit from a single technology idea.[28]

In well-educated, evolving societies, as more knowledge-based products are introduced into the market place, the traditional three economic essentials of land, labor, and capital-intensive industries exert less leverage on the domestic economy.

In countries with a free democratic tradition, the investment in knowledge-based technologies over the past 20 years is one of the key reasons for the stable, growing economies they enjoyed in the late 1990s. Such investment is a key enabler for Free Market Fusion entrepreneurship.

The Sum of Our Choices

Where will these upheavals lead us in the coming decade, and in the coming century? French author and philosopher Albert Camus observed that, as individuals, we are the sum of our choices. And so we will be as a global village. We inhabit a world that offers us the tools with which to wield superhuman direction over our future.

While clearly we cannot control change, we can, through our commitment to life-enhancing policies and choices, attempt to orchestrate its movement. We have the opportunity, and the responsibility, to choose from the array of possible futures the one which we believe will best contribute to the forward progress of civilization and the greater freedom of humanity. Although it is arrogant to assume that we can have detailed control of our future, it is intelligently selfish to distill value, and to prioritize goals for our future.

In order to direct this future, however, we must learn how to balance the competing demands of stewardship versus growth, community versus diversity, people versus profits, and government versus the private sector. There is no reason to assume that in the future these considerations cannot be complementary. However, it will require rethinking many of our most intransigent, and least examined, assumptions. Also, it will require new restraints at every level.

Defining the Education Race

The future of the earth and its fragile inhabitants is being determined by what our children are learning in their classrooms. How do we educate our children for a world whose only consistency is change? Can we teach them to maintain the earth by finding a sustainable relationship between economics and ecology? What skills must we teach them to prepare them for a productive life, to help them help America compete in a global marketplace? How can we enable them to safeguard the environment they live in and to accept and respect the diversity of people, cultures, and ideologies that will define the world? What we teach our children will determine whether or not they will succeed.

First, we must teach them *how to embrace change.* We must help them to develop the internal balance and underlying stability of values and confidence that will enable them to see in a constantly changing world not crisis, but opportunity. As parents, goes the old adage, we strive to give our children roots and wings. Never were those two qualities in more demand than they will be in the coming decades. Both will be central to the resiliency our children must develop in order to thrive. However, used innovatively and wisely, our children's own media (television, the Internet, Nintendo style CDs and similar edutainment technologies) can become powerful allies in the effort to teach them the skills necessary to navigate change. To ignore these tools is folly. It is sacrificing our children on the cross of vested interests who often resist change to preserve their own turf.

Second, we must teach them *how to learn*, for lifelong learning will facilitate the intellectual openness necessary to adapt to advances in information and technology.

The march of the twin columns of information and technology into 21st century life will be relentless. As pointed out by Marvin Cetron and Owen Davies in *American Renaissance*, the sheer enormity of the information resources available to children born in the last 10 years requires some radical adjustments in how they are taught, and how information must be prepared for access:

> "By the time today's kindergartners graduate from high school, the amount of information in the world will have doubled four times.
>
> The Class of 2010 will be exposed to more information in one year than their grandparents encountered in their entire lives.
>
> The Class of 2010 will have to assimilate more inventions and more new information than have appeared in the last 150 years.
>
> By 2010, there will be hardly a job in this country that does not require skill in using powerful computers and telecommunications systems."[29]

I would add schools, and the teaching/learning process, cannot remain unchanged.

Third, we must teach them *how to use electronic tools* to extend the capabilities of their intellect, in the same way that electronic tools extend the capabilities of today's workforce. How we use the technological tools at our disposal will dramatically impact how effectively we cope with the challenges of the future.

Today's educational technologies include telecourses, courses and degree programs on the Internet, computers, interactive video discs, on-line databases and access to libraries, multi-media experiences in the new cyberschools' environments, and virtual reality. All have opened up a wealth of learning alternatives. These alternatives must become an integral part of the learning experience, both in the classroom and outside.

More and more educators are embracing this reality and are committed to using advanced educational technologies to enrich and extend the learning experience. These are the teachers who will lead our students into the 21st century. Those teachers who choose not to embrace this reality will simply be left behind by their students' superior technology skills; they are the ones who will help create the "peasants" of the knowledge culture.

Last, and perhaps most importantly, we must help our children learn *how to think creatively*, to think beyond the boundaries of what is known for they will be the Free Market Fusion entrepreneurs of tomorrow. Although connecting with intellectual activities of the past is important, many of the solutions of the past will be inadequate for the complexities of the 21st century.

The Cold War's arms race is over. The nations of the world are now in an education race. This is one any country could lose easily by resisting change and protecting the vested interests of some in the education establishment. New models for education excellence and professional training are ignored at great peril.

In order to succeed, our children will have to be skilled at perceiving and functioning within emerging patterns, shifting social structures, and an ever-changing architecture of international relationships. Their world will be shaped by new constituencies, new challenges, and the necessity for new systems. They will face unfamiliar, rocky paths with little but their attitudes, their value system, their education, their native intelligence, and their belief in themselves and their compatriots to be able to fashion workable solutions.

America faced similar challenges over 200 years ago and managed to produce the Declaration of Independence, the Bill of Rights, and the Constitution. In the 21st century, new models of entrepreneurship for business, government and education will be necessary for democratic progress in all free societies.

An Interview with David Osborne

Osborne is co-author of *Reinventing Government* and *Banishing Bureaucracy*.

Is an important part of reinventing government to privatize as many functions of government as possible?

Osborne: I wouldn't say it that way. Part of reinventing government is to find the most effective vehicles or combinations, and that can be profits and non-profits together, government and non-profits, government and for-profits and so forth. Then you identify the part that is missing competition. But privatization is a means, not an end. There are many ways to invite in the private sector to government. And sometimes the private sector can't do what the public sector has to do.

What are weaknesses or pitfalls to the privatization approach?

Osborne: A big pitfall is privatizing by turning functions over to a private monopoly. These are sometimes just a little better or a little worse than the public monopoly, but it's not a good way to reinvent. You still have to put considerable energy into the contracting-out process, and this is work that the public organization sometimes forgets has to be done when the decision is made to seek outside providers. Also, the public entity does lose the ability to exercise certain kinds of control. With certain functions, such as operating a prison, if things start to go wrong you can't just step in and re-assert control. And, business people should realize there are certain things the public just does not want to put in private hands, such as police, the courts, and the military. There have been times when mercenary armies were used, but in most developed countries today, this isn't regarded as a good way to go.

How can entrepreneurs in government remain entrepreneurs and survive, even after leading a successful crusade for change?

Osborne: In my company, we use (Peter) Drucker's definition of an entrepreneur, which he borrowed from Jean Baptiste: "The entrepreneur shifts resources out of an area of lower and into an area of higher productivity and greater yield." That's a broad definition, and by that definition, every public manager ought to be an entrepreneur. But most aren't. Part of reinventing government is changing the culture of organizations. When you find yourself in an organization that doesn't appreciate you, leave. I give this counsel frequently. But people aren't trapped, and working for government isn't some form of slavery, especially in strong job markets like we have now.

How can an entrepreneur outside government identify privatization or partnership advocates within government with whom to network?

Osborne: It's like finding any kind of business partner. Keep your eyes and ears open, ask, make phone calls, go out to lunch with people you want to get to know. Wander around the public sector, go to public meetings and forums. Keep alert. There's no magic to it, but it's not hard, either.

How can an entrepreneur inside government identify possible partners outside government without creating a conflict of interest?

Osborne: The important thing is to do informal networking. But, when the process is ready to go to the next step, then the person inside government has to be careful to revert to formal procedures, such as requests for proposals and formal contracting bids.

Can you provide a good example of efforts that have both reduced regulation of business and simplified government?

Osborne: The Office of Safety and Health Administration (OSHA) began an experiment with businesses in Maine in 1993 that has been a great success. OSHA administrators realized that their normal process of rules and fines just didn't work, especially when they could only get around to re-visiting businesses every 9 or 10 years. They also realized that safety didn't always have to involve more rules. So they took several large employers and told them that OSHA would back off if management would create labor-management safety groups and show an improvement in safety records. The companies jumped on it, their records did improve, and it's been a good example of how people can work together. There have been similar examples at the U.S. Environmental Protection Agency. It just shows that government can win compliance from the private sector by asking for cooperation, rather than assuming an adversarial approach.

CHAPTER 5

ENTREPRENEURS AS INVENTORS
How innovation drives Free Market Fusion

A Swiss physicist and author, Theodore Modis, recently gave a most unique view of American entrepreneurship and economic trends. When asked to demonstrate how his particular theory of business and economic growth fits into a predictable mathematical S-curve (a variation of the bell curve), he offered the view that many of our most entrepreneurial companies were, essentially, organizations in the right place at the right time.

Modis said, in essence, that companies such as Microsoft, Apple, IBM and Oracle would have appeared and soared to their high levels of success without Bill Gates, Steve Jobs, Tom Watson and Larry Ellison.

The underpinning of Modis' theory is that the entrepreneurial climate has been so strong and dominant, other personalities or combinations of leaders would have appeared to form similar enterprises to meet society's market demands.

Applying Modis' theory gives us an additional tool with which to assess Free Market Fusion opportunities.

It's a theory which bears further study (see Modis' complete comments in the interview at the end of Chapter 7), and we have to wonder how it would hold up to such unique inventiveness and entrepreneurship as exemplified by Thomas Edison. Modis' apparent explanation is that there were other inventor-entrepreneurs lurking in the wings who eventually would have produced all of Edison's inventions. The time was ripe, and the climate of science and industriousness, in the U.S. in particular, made those inventions inevitable.

Edison, usually cited as the greatest inventor in history, had received almost 1,100 patents by the time of his death in 1931. He invented the electric light, the phonograph, a mimeograph machine, the first electronic vote-counter, an improved stock ticker, and a type of motion-picture camera and projector called the "Kinetoscope." In addition, he influenced the future of the telephone, radio, and television industries through his scientific and engineering genius.

Although his talent was in scientific discovery, Edison's entrepreneurial passion drove him to focus on areas that would lead to practical solutions, products, or services responsive to marketplace needs. His mimeograph, or "electric pen" device, was created, patented, and marketed under his direct supervision, including the advertising copy.[30] Besides sharing the profits with his key assistants, Edison plowed much of the money back into his laboratory work to pursue electric lighting, the phonograph, and other inventions. He was quick to understand that the licensing, patenting, and sharing of technology could generate even more successes if managed properly.

In these pursuits, he was supremely successful in a Free Market Fusion-style of entrepreneurship. He succeeded at his own goals and also made an overwhelming contribution to the improvement of daily life.

It is arguable that Edison's near-superhuman productivity (averaging about two patentable devices for every month of his adult life) was a direct result of the fact that he was in the United States, where he was not hindered by class and government restrictions.

A majority of the country's founding fathers believed that individual reward should correspond proportionately to individual effort and success, and that economic freedom would bring forth the best efforts of the American people. Both history and current events have proved them right. Between 1800 and 1900, Americans invented, perfected, patented, and/or built and marketed:

- the automatic reaper (Cyrus McCormick),

- the repeating revolver (Samuel Colt),

- The Pullman sleeping car (George Pullman),

- the first airbrake for trains (George Westinghouse),

- the first practical typewriter (Christopher Latham Sholes, Carlos Glidden, and Samuel W. Soule),

- the telegraph (Samuel Morse),

- the telephone (Alexander Graham Bell),

- elevators, (Elisha Graves Otis and his sons), and

- the Linotype typesetting machine (Ottmar Mergenthaler).

Additionally, advances in the use of machine tools and interchangeable parts continued the pace of technological change during this period.

The railroad, telegraph, telephone, textile, steel, electric, and oil industries sprang to life during this same period. They were fueled by the vision, drive, and ambitions of such men as Francis Cabot Lowell, Andrew Carnegie, J.P. Morgan, and John D. Rockefeller, who saw opportunities in change and rushed to seize them. Although the worst excesses of entrepreneurialism, such as anti-competitive, monopolistic behavior, also surfaced (and were curbed) during this era, it was nevertheless one of the most dynamic periods of human history.

20ᵗʰ Century Contributions

The 20ᵗʰ century has differed radically in its characteristics, but not in its innovations. Although the challenges have changed, the drive to create new products and solutions continues as powerfully as before.

In the first fifty years of this century alone, scientists, inventors, and entrepreneurs brought us airplanes; silent, then "talking," movies; tea bags; the $850 Model T, whose low price made cars affordable for the public; farm tractors; electric frying pans; the artificial fiber called "nylon;" Band-Aids; xerography; helicopters; frozen foods; the first practical electronic computer (ENIAC); transistors to replace vacuum tubes and a dazzling array of other complex and practical technological advances.

During the same period, Ford revolutionized the automobile industry (any many others) with his application of mass production and standardization to the manufacturing process. His production system became so efficient that by 1926 the price of his 1908 $850 car had dropped to $310.

Ford was not alone. Theodore Vail drove the development of America's long distance telephone communications network through his ambitions for AT&T. Visionary David Sarnoff at RCA understood the implications of wireless communications and shepherded in first the radio and then television broadcast industries, now reaching out across international boundaries. The Watsons of IBM, Thomases Sr. and Jr., fought to overcome initial industry reluctance to market computers to businesses, and eventually earned IBM decades of leadership in the international and domestic computer industries.

The entrepreneurial instinct continues unabated, and it now has spread from America's garage laboratories and temporary office suites to the thriving technology centers of Shanghai and Prague.

Track Record for the '80s and '90s

More than 931,000 U.S. patents were granted from 1980 through 1995.[31] Between 1985 and 1995, more than 1.8 million new businesses were started, and billions of dollars of venture capital invested across America.[32] As the parameters of the U.S. and world economies have shifted — from domestic to international, from industrialized to information-based — businesses and scientists have been the leaders in the search for ways to create better, faster, smarter, more efficient products and services to win global markets.

Competitive capitalism, as defined by Milton Friedman in his 1962 book *Capitalism and Freedom,* is "a free private enterprise exchange economy," and has been the structure under which innovation and entrepreneurship most effectively flourish.[33]

Certainly this has been the case for the industry with which I am most familiar, the cable television industry. Cable entrepreneurs, many of whom literally strung the first wires with their own hands from their own trucks, created, *without significant government help or taxpayers' dollars,* tremendous financial expansion. This includes over a hundred thousand jobs and a myriad of television-based entertainment and education alternatives — in sum, a new, stunningly successful industry.

Cable entrepreneurs are now charting the next territory, a transformation into a new convergent industry that will create and expand new services to its subscribers and its communities. This redefinition and reinvestment can best take place where government interference is minimal.

Defining and Using Strengths

How do we allocate our resources in order to address our needs? We must search for a way to integrate the moral imperative of equality of opportunity, upon which modern democracies were founded, with the social and economic imperative of meritocracy, of finding and nurturing the best and the brightest, without which a democracy may not survive. Both approaches are necessary; history makes clear that either without the other will lead us down a road of devastation and despair.

Democratic nations face a choice: they can grow into their weaknesses, or they can grow into their strengths. These strengths include:

A cultural acceptance of creative, imaginative thinking that breaks through the normal boundaries of established ideas and structures. Entrepreneurs have succeeded so spectacularly because they've learned that sometimes when wisdom becomes conventional, it ceases to be wise. Like Ted Turner and his original team of top executives at CNN, they've learned to look far beyond the "wisdom" of entrenched interests to see different realities, and therefore radically different possibilities.

When the three broadcast networks *knew* there was no market for news beyond their nightly half-hour newscasts, Ted Turner declined to accept this conventional wisdom. He decided instead to launch Atlanta-based CNN with an intrepid band of dedicated reporters, producers, writers, engineers, and the support of cable operators, thereby out-witting conventional wisdom and revolutionizing broadcast journalism in the process.[34]

An ability to thrive in the midst of disorder, and downright chaos. Entrepreneurs are not only able to survive change, they have historically embraced it for the opportunities provided. Austrian Joseph Schumpeter was the first economist to identify the impact of entrepreneurial activity on a nation's economy. In 1942, Schumpeter observed in *Capitalism, Socialism, and Democracy*:

> The function of entrepreneurs is to reform or revolutionize the pattern of production by exploiting an invention or, more generally, an untried technological possibility for producing a new commodity or producing an old one in a new way, by opening up a new source of supply of materials or a new outlet for products, by reorganizing an industry and so on.[35]

An eagerness to exploit technological advances in the service of new solutions. Consumers have embraced an onslaught of products whose capabilities represent the merging of technological advances with established functions. The Internet, computerized vehicles, voice mail, interactive educational technologies, medical imaging devices, cable television's information and education services, and the integration of robotics into old-line manufacturing processes are but a few examples of technological solutions accepted by developed societies.

How developed societies *use* technology in the future will become a critical question. We have in the past viewed technology in terms of products: developing new products for new markets. In the future, however, experts predict that innovation will be more effectively (and competitively) undertaken in terms of *process*. We will need to fuse different technologies together in order to achieve more efficient processes, and more efficient use of resources, human capital, knowledge, and imagination.

A belief in diversity as a strengthening rather than destructive societal element. A nation of immigrants, America has profited from the intellects and energies of its citizens to an extent unimaginable to societies steeped in the constraining assumptions of racial or societal purity. The earlier list of inventions credited to Americans over the past two hundred years quickly reveals the major contributions made by individuals who left their native lands to pursue their lives and professions in an arena of intellectual and personal freedom.

Certainly there are difficulties inherent in diversity; in fact, part of the struggle our public school systems are confronting is how to educate children whose cultural backgrounds, not to mention languages, reflect the vast variety to be found throughout all the countries of the world. In the early 1990s, students in the Los Angeles County School District spoke a total of 80 languages.

While diversity must be acknowledged and honored, we also must focus on our common ties. "The economic evidence about immigration," notes author James Fallows, a former staff writer and Asia correspondent for *The Atlantic Monthly* and former editor of *U.S. News and World Report*, "...is open and shut. Immigrants are disproportionately entrepreneurial, determined, and adaptable, and through history they have strengthened the economy of whatever society they join."[36]

A fundamental confidence in mankind's ability to overcome obstacles through applied intellect. Thomas Jefferson, a man renowned not only for his impressive intellect, but for his equally impressive intellectual tolerance stated, "I have sworn upon the altar of God eternal hostility against every form of tyranny over the mind of man." To the best of our abilities, Americans generally have sought to honor his oath.

This dedication to freedom has resulted in a commitment to equality of access to education. The results are no less than phenomenal. As products of this open education philosophy, America's 5.5 million scientists and engineers have between them garnered more Nobel prizes than all of the rest of world combined. Not only that, but the U.S. model of free democratic capitalism is now being adapted all over the world. We have a tradition of invention, innovation, and ingenuity, a history of success, and an irrepressible belief that we're the good guys. Taken together, these characteristics result in a nation convinced that it can take on any challenge and succeed.

It was these strengths that propelled America into an internationally recognized leadership position within fifty years of its inception. It was these strengths that enabled the American economic machine to become the envy of the entire world in the years following World War II. It will be these strengths that undergird our efforts in the 21st century to fuse our resources into a new architecture of achievement, one based not on diminishing capacities but rather on expanding possibilities. It was these strengths Woodrow Wilson had in mind when he stated, "I believe in democracy because it releases the energy of every human being."

Rediscovering Our Strengths

Americans confront daily the increasing ability of other nations to compete. Up until the mid-1990s it became tempting — even in vogue — to look to those nations, most especially Japan, for "solutions" to reverse America's decline in market leadership.

However, just as a spate of books and films arrived bolstering the image of Japanese supremacy, the Japanese real estate market collapsed, precipitating a banking crisis. This evolved into a long-term financial downturn in that country, the worst since the years immediately after World War II. By the fall of 1997, just when it seemed that the Japanese government was finally taking measures to resolve its seven-year crisis, the financial crevasse suddenly widened as the economies of Thailand, South Korea, Indonesia and to a lesser extent all the rest of East Asia, with the exception of China, began to unravel.

Suddenly, Asian sacrifice, hard work and dedication to traditional principles of Confucianism seemed to falter as a surrogate for Western-style free markets and entrepreneurship, not to mention Western democratic-style government.

James Fallows has written two books assessing Asian development and how it measures up to American experience and industriousness. In *More Like Us* (1989), he argues eloquently that Americans are better served by simply recommitting to their inherent national strengths:

> "Different societies have different ways of creating...cultural conditions for economic growth and political stability. America is perfectly capable of doing so; after all, it is still one of the world's great success stories. But it can't do it the way in which Japanese or Korean or Chinese or German or Swedish culture does. Other societies, most of all Japan, can match individual self-interest with the collective social good by using tools that America does not and cannot possess. If we have to out-cooperate and out-sacrifice the Japanese, we may as well quit. We need, instead, to find our own tools."[37]

In *Looking at the Sun* (1994), Fallows continued his journal of the Asian spectacle by looking at the economies and social fabrics throughout the Asian world, and how they are tied irrevocably to Japan. And just as firm is the mistaken American tendency he describes of insisting on analyzing the other Asian powerhouses in strictly Western terms, beginning with the historical tendency to regard other cultures and countries as fertile ground for political and religious conversion — indeed, of a cultural make-over to "be" more like Americans.[38] When will they convert to true Western capitalism and democracy? When will their governments remove themselves from protectionist roles?

By December 1997, Fallows was reflecting on quite another Asian spectacle, as the stock markets in Hong Kong, Bangkok and Seoul slid into desperate turmoil. Writing in *U.S. News and World Report*, Fallows offered the following perspective on Asia's reversal of fortunes:

> "The 'Asian economic model,' which since the 1960s has brought more people out of poverty faster than ever before in human history, was built on the trinity of over-investment, over-saving, and over-guidance....The choice now being made in Asia is how much of its development model to discard...[the model's] aim has been to use savings and exports to build industry and thereby to create high-income jobs. Judged by those standards, it is quite far from having failed. In major manufacturing categories, Japanese, Korean, and Chinese manufacturers have held or expanded world market share even as banks collapsed around them. The cultural underpinnings of the Asian system — education, discipline, thrift — are as robust as ever..."[39]

And how will the Asian entrepreneur fare in this new, less optimistic environment? That remains to be seen, though the high savings rates — often 30 percent or more — of families and small family-owned enterprises in Asia could be one factor that helps cushion the free-fall of the markets there and hasten a recovery.

Whether Free Market Fusion can survive in Asia depends on many factors, such as the willingness of governments and large institutions to encourage business innovation.

Clearly, one of America's special tools is the entrepreneur. Existing in a free-enterprise environment, they are challenged constantly to grow, to adapt, to re-envision their missions and to re-conceptualize their constituencies. That they have been able to maintain their viability in the midst of an onslaught of change is an indication of the amazing strength and resiliency of America's many institutions.

In this vein, it will be fascinating to see how the countries of Europe choose to handle their differences and their unique strengths as they move toward a true common economic market. Additionally, it may be that the changing arena will provide an opportunity for European financial, cultural, educational, and social institutions, to demonstrate to American institutions how to navigate successfully and effectively in uncharted waters.

While the specter of economic uncertainty looms large in the late 1990s, history has shown that such conditions produce a continuing stream of Free Market Fusion opportunities for the willing entrepreneur.

As he traveled across America during 1831 and 1832, Alexis de Tocqueville was struck repeatedly by the impression that Americans were in a constant state of motion. Describing this phenomena in *Democracy in America,* the author and historian noted:

> "The universal movement prevailing in the United States, the frequent reversals of fortune, and the unexpected shifts in public and private wealth all unite to keep the mind in a sort of feverish agitation which wonderfully disposes it toward every type of exertion and keeps it, so to say, above the common level of humanity. For an American the whole of life is treated like a game of chance, a time of revolution, or the day of a battle."[40]

In the 21st century, it will be the capacity of citizens living in democracies to adapt to change, to accommodate constant "disorder," that will fuel their abilities to innovate and to achieve goals. These same criteria will determine the success or failure of both for-profit and nonprofit organizations, which must change their management structures if they are going to move quickly and effectively. In this effort, Free Market Fusion is a process that has an important role.

An Interview with James Fallows

Fallows is author of *More Like Us* and *Looking at the Sun*, as well as several other books on U.S. current affairs and the media.

In the decade since you wrote *More Like Us*, we have seen a progressive — and now, suddenly, radically different — Asian economic picture unfold, from riches to declining markets and default. How do you see the differences between Americans and Japanese in terms of the way they handle economic damage control and recovery, and any changes in their self-perceptions? Are the Asians any more contrite, and are Americans any more detached in their self-assessments?

Fallows: I feel abashed in offering generalizations about "Asian" attitudes to stresses of this sort, since so many different cultures have so many different traits. Traditional Malays describe themselves as being fatalistic about adversity, while seeing the ethnic Chinese in their midst as more resilient, for example.

But I think between America and Japan, one contrast is fair to note. On the whole, Japanese culture prides itself on stoicism — an ability to withstand real hardship and sacrifice. Thus it takes pride in its recovery from the horrors of defeat and the indignity of post-war occupation. American culture, I would say, features instead an optimistic "things will get better" spirit. After a bankruptcy, after a divorce, after being laid off, people are encouraged to think that the next venture they start will turn out well. In practice, both of these ethics can equip people to bounce back from difficulties, but they do so in different ways.

More Like Us comments on what you call "creative destruction" in regard to both U.S. and China societies, and gives us reason to believe that the seeds of entrepreneurship can originate in a racially homogenous totalitarian country (China) or in a multi-cultural democratic system (U.S.). Is China's future role to become the "Superman" of innovation and enterprise, the center of new entrepreneurship and the spawning ground for new ideas and inventions, replacing the American tradition in that role? From a 1998 view, will China perhaps become the most capitalistic of all?

Fallows: First, about the premise of the question: while China as a whole has a sense of racial specialness and separateness from the West, I would not think of it as a racially homogenous country. There are huge differences north to south, east to west. Nonetheless, it's clearly true that this culture does reward many "American" style productive traits, from a practical problem-solving orientation to a desire for each person to have his own (or family's) enterprise. The market tradition seemed not to be extinguished even during the Mao years. Whether in the long run this is destined to be *the* most capitalistic society, I couldn't say, nor could anyone, I think, since so many historic, military, and other factors are involved. But their prospects are good.

Regarding the Japanese perspective of "common good of the people first" that you mention in both your books, do you sense any stress fractures in this outlook, especially among younger Japanese who have come of age in the past 5-7 years and have to deal with the economic problems caused by their predecessors and elders? Are they perhaps becoming more independent and entrepreneurial in spirit as a result?

Fallows: I am sure that changes in both directions are underway; the question is the rate of change, compared to how robust the traits are. It is possible that today's economic strains really will erode them. On the other hand, it's worth remembering that outsiders have consistently overestimated the rate of change on these fronts. We'll just have to watch and see.

Why does the entrepreneurial spirit you describe in *Looking at the Sun* survive and thrive so strongly in China, but seems not to have made the narrow leap to Japan?

Fallows: Here is one guess: China has been so large and populous for so long that an "every man for himself," or really "every family for itself" spirit has been necessary. Japan has thought of itself as small and contained enough to be run with a more group-conscious spirit. Also, as a number of cultural historians point out (most recently Sheldon Garon, in *Molding Japanese Minds*), there have been concerted efforts by Japanese public officials for a century or more to promote the collective spirit. This emphasis may have dampened the entrepreneurial potential of the country.

Can the tradition of high personal savings rates in most Asian cultures help mitigate the current financial crisis? Is this a factor, or did it drop by the wayside over the past decade in countries such as South Korea, Thailand and Indonesia?

Fallows: Yes, this will make a huge difference — and does help explain the different predicaments of different Asian countries. Taiwan, Japan, and Singapore have VERY high savings rates — and they are the three in least urgent distress during the financial crisis. (Japan has tremendous stagnation, but not Indonesia-style collapse). Indonesia and Malaysia and Thailand are much less frugal in this sense, and are walking on thinner ice.

Will the Asian economic recovery likely include more or less government regulation of economic policies in the respective countries, or are we likely to see yet another set of economic models that are still quite different from the Western free market philosophy?

Fallows: My guess is: A quite significant long-term difference in Asian and Western models. It is possible that the two approaches really will converge. But the cultures, histories, and social preferences of many Asian societies differ enough from America's to make long-term difference possible, too.

CHAPTER 6

FREE MARKET FUSION TOOLS: SCANNING

The best way I know to discover Free Market Fusion opportunities is to engage in a constant process of scanning. It's a technique I've been employing and refining for years. Other executives I know use their own forms of scanning to keep abreast of trends and opportunities.

Scanning and using the results to build a knowledge base is represented in Stage 1 of the Free Market Fusion process. However, it is an implicit activity throughout the life of any venture and is ongoing in all stages.

Although scanning is more art form than science, it generally breaks down into two primary pursuits:

(1) formal media and literature monitoring; and

(2) informal personal observation.

Formal scanning can be aided by the corporate library or various forms of information services groups, but the key to it is the constant application of imagination and wide-ranging reading and awareness. My general recommendations for setting up this process are offered later in this chapter.

According to *Webster's Encyclopedic Unabridged Dictionary of the English Language*, scanning has two distinct, but contradictory, primary meanings, hence the need for the further definitions:

(1) *to examine minutely; scrutinize carefully;* and

(2) *to glance at or read hastily.*

In this book, it means any type of scanning activity. What follows is a further description of the types of scanning activity. (The illustration on page 111, Figure 5, shows how these techniques flow together and build on one another to help build the knowledge base shown in Figure 2.)

To scan meaningfully, irreverence is required. Think in terms of resolutions, not barriers. Focus on solutions and work to resolve barriers that prevent solutions. Think backwards from solutions, not forward from problems. There is ambiguity here, but living with confusion, partial answers, and seeming inconsistencies is common in the Free Market Fusion process.

Look for new combinations of things, not only of entities but of functions and activities. Beware of conventional wisdom. As Albert Einstein said, "Imagination is more important than knowledge."

Ambient or present tense scanning. This is a surface scan. It is first on the list because you can begin it anytime, anywhere, even right now.

Figure 5

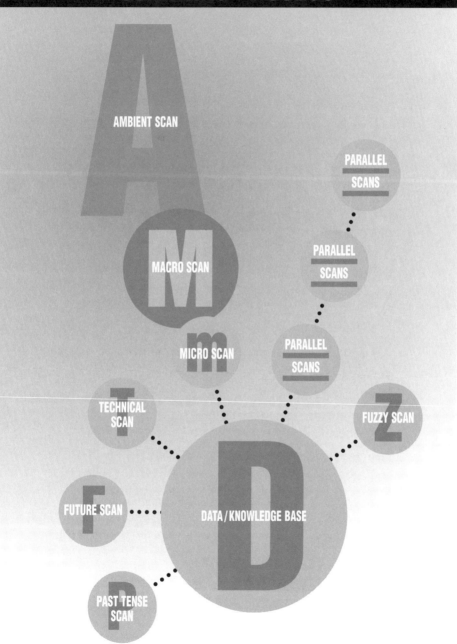

SCANNING PROCESS

AMBIENT SCAN

PARALLEL SCANS

MACRO SCAN

PARALLEL SCANS

MICRO SCAN

PARALLEL SCANS

TECHNICAL SCAN

FUZZY SCAN

FUTURE SCAN

DATA / KNOWLEDGE BASE

PAST TENSE SCAN

Ambient scanning is best described as a quick snapshot of what you see currently, such as the immediate images, conversations, information, emotional responses to situations and how you see the world interacting in the present tense. Just follow your nose.

I want to emphasize just how important the informal aspect of ambient scanning is to your Free Market Fusion intelligence gathering effort. Many people tend to discount this, adopting the attitude that if the information doesn't arrive via in-box or e-mail, it doesn't count. "Luck" in the field of business opportunity often can be traced back to an alert listener or person who was willing to initiate a conversation when it would have been easier to be reticent.

First-hand observation is a scanning activity that no one else can do for you. Take note of everything around you: What people are wearing, the radio stations they listen to, music, food items on grocery store shelves, what people are buying at checkout stands, the titles of books being read on subways, categories of magazines and their placement on news stands as well as the content of magazines, what sections left-behind newspapers are opened to, what people do for recreation, how movie theater lobbies are being redecorated, what types of retail establishments and night spots are opening up across the street from hotels, and topics of interest when you visit your old college professor. Try to stay as much in the present as possible.

Observe, watch, listen, remember, and keep a personal journal or organized random notes, preferably on a laptop computer, that can be part of your knowledge database. Tune in. Be a sponge. It's all part of the scan.

Macro scanning. This is a far-reaching examination of situations or environments, a study of the "big picture." It is more careful and thorough, and employs many of the media and information sources listed later in this chapter. Broad scale is the important perspective here. You are moving rapidly through massive information, looking for trends and opportunities. When you think you may have spotted something, make note of it and keep moving. You can do a microscan later.

Micro scanning. This narrows the examination down to select topics, situations or categories. It also involves more careful study, but it is more "vertical" than macro scanning, because you have narrowed your subject down and are learning everything possible about it. You are drilling down into more and more specifics. Even though you are being rational and organized, you still follow your instincts here as you narrow your focus.

Technology scanning. This involves focusing on technology implications, including technology evolution, innovation and applications. If you are a technology buff, it will be second nature. If you don't normally pay attention to technology developments, you can do it by watching closely for gadgets arriving on the market, checking out new product reviews in your favorite magazines, observing what types of technology related magazines and books are taking up space on newsstands and in bookstores, or stopping by the annual new car or computer and electronic exhibitions that travel the country. This process can be macro or micro depending on where you think you are headed.

Future-tense scanning. This is a combination of assembling clues and hints about what might happen in the future with an imaginary "walk-about" into the future. This depends on knowledge acquired thus far, but must incorporate flights of fantasy. You must project the present and evolve it into a future time frame.

Future tense scanning is also advisable if you wish to project the time at which a needed piece of technology will arrive, or if a need will increase or decrease in intensity and size. One way to do this is to relax, then let your imagination walk out into the future five, ten, or perhaps twenty years, and do the best you can to imagine and visualize what the world looks like at that time. Although your assessments will be based upon your assimilated information level (the information you currently hold from education, experience, social relationships, data accumulation, scanning and other sources), try to let your imagination run free, unchain it. Imagination is important here.

One of the outgrowths of this process can be a strategic planning or scenario development process, as explained in Chapter 7. In this process, the same group takes a long-view approach to the "What if?" question and considers possibilities and even improbabilities that daily business operations rarely allow for. While this activity was long considered a frivolous pursuit by some senior managers, more recently it has gained favor as key individuals have looked for ways — any way possible — to gain an edge on their competitors. Scenario planning follows research and depends upon it. This is dealt with in more detail in the next chapter.

Past-tense scanning. This is the well-known hindsight technique of looking at what successful processes were used in the past, as well as strategies that didn't work. Obviously this is much more precise than future-tense, but you need to be careful to look for possible solutions that weren't tried in the past and may only be sketchily documented. The question "Why not?" needs to be posed frequently in past-tense scanning.

Past-tense scanning also can be helpful in instances where you are looking for resolution models (what successful processes were deployed to address similar situations in the past?) or recurring opportunities. Obviously, with the availability of computerized databases and the recorded knowledge in books and periodicals, past-tense scanning lends itself to greater precision than does future-tense.

Fuzzy scanning. This is typically a focus on just part of the scanning environment, ignoring the negatives, or adding in different factors — such as posing a competitor as a partner. Again, concentrate on solutions, not problems. In fact, when you begin fuzzy scanning it helps to ignore problems (you can come back to them later). Think in terms of sculpting fog and molding silly putty. Envision the desired result and think back from there. This is highly subjective, but can produce some useful and interesting possibilities for business approaches and combinations.

There are many types of scanning, and those who engage in the scanning process create their own tools. For example, I have found that fuzzy scanning can be used for a more general approach, especially if you want to overlook paradoxes or conflicts when scanning for entities that might contribute to a Free Market Fusion undertaking.

Parallel scanning. This is also known as intangible leverage, and means getting others involved in scanning for you, simultaneously but independently. Candidates who may be willing to do scanning for you include work associates, friends, applicable experts or perhaps a business professor giving an assignment to a class of students on your behalf. I have had very good luck with imaginative research librarians.

The Best Filter is You

On the more conventional level, it is crucial to keep abreast of news media, books, journals, newsletters, academic and research reports, TV broadcasts, and electronic information originals, such as the new electronic magazines and newsletters that appear exclusively on the Internet.

Getting help is fine, but stay very involved. Turning this over to someone down the chain of command immediately puts obstacles between yourself and the most important information. One of the main purposes of the scanning mission is to discover new information that may spark a connection or open a new vista that no one else would even dream about. You don't know what you don't know; how can someone else? Do as much of the process yourself as possible, within reason.

If you are in a position where you can allocate the budget, retain an outside professional with a background in library science, journalism, or general business research to prepare a reading folder from sources that you pick. I do this, and I find it very helpful, but I supply direction to the process.

If you get help, it should be someone with a genuine love and interest in information and in ferreting out obscure and seemingly mundane tidbits of information. Alternatives include using a college intern or a student relative who needs a part-time job. When you start using the concept you will find your own resources from among your own acquaintances and contacts. Again, remember imagination is important.

It's perfectly okay if there's absolutely no money, and no one to do it but yourself. Spend two Saturday mornings a month in the local college library. Ask the reference staff for search tips and to keep an eye out for the areas of interest to you. Then dig in. You'll get to see everything fresh and untainted, and what you'll learn can be worth an MBA several times over.

My own company employs the services of various information professionals, including a research librarian, to provide much of this information. However, for smaller organizations or for an individual, there are many techniques for information scanning and database development that can be employed at minimal or no cost.

Treat your scanning process as a unique and personal pursuit, and don't let it become so formal that it loses its comfort level. Your mind needs to be relaxed, and your subconscious needs to be assigned scanning tasks as well. There are numerous clipping and information search services offering packaged information, but they should be considered as a supplement to what you need.

Introduce yourself to a business or reference librarian and, perhaps over lunch or coffee, explain your interests and objectives. This person could end up being your paid scanning consultant, and may even be willing to give free advice. Often these professionals are information "wonks" who can give you plenty of direction on using the resources they deal with on a regular basis.

Information Overload is a Myth

I'd like to offer one more observation. For certain people it may be an admonition, but if that's the case it's highly unlikely they have picked up this book. There is a growing chorus of complaints about "information overload" brought about by the information revolution. I disagree. We are just peeking under the corner of the blanket cloaking the world's information potential, and getting a glimpse of what treasures await us. We don't need less information, we only need more intelligent ways to organize, select, and use it.

To the iconoclasts who say there is too much, I would question their sense of adventure and curiosity. I would charge them with a failure to apply discipline, and with a lack of self confidence (or willingness) to carefully focus, decipher, and select what they need. At the outset, scanning has everything to do with quantity, meaning a very general cognizance of the blur of events and information passing by. At the end, it has everything to do with focus and quality.

The informed scanner doesn't try to absorb the entire world's information output every few days. A cooking metaphor is useful here, because the result of creating and executing a successful scanning recipe is the difference between gourmet dining on carefully selected information and malnourishment with too much junk data. One approach will lead to discovery and analysis of viable Free Market Fusion opportunities. The other will lead to a predictable and somewhat mediocre menu of business ideas and confusion.

You can make your own list. Here are some recommendations for scanning resources to get started:

Books:

Statistical Abstract of the U.S. (U.S. Government Printing Office)

Business Periodicals Index

Dun & Bradstreet Million Dollar Directory

Directory of World Politics

Reader's Guide To Periodicals (Print, CD-ROM or On-line)

Ulrich's Newsletter Index

The World Almanac (annual)

Encyclopedia Britannica (Print or On-Line)

Webster's Encyclopedic Unabridged Dictionary

The Art of Being Well Informed, by Andrew P. Garvin (see interview at the end of this chapter)

Periodicals:

American Demographics (tries to make sense out of the rapidly shifting trends and whims of North American consumer tastes and how to quantify them)

The Economist (arguably the best international source for general, business, technology and financial news on a weekly basis)

Foreign Affairs (the thought behind main-stream international policy events)

Future Survey (newsletter of The World Future Society)

Harper's (often reports on mainstream topics using first-hand or somewhat unorthodox sources; predictably liberal on some issues, but surprisingly iconoclastic and anti-big government on others)

Manchester Guardian Weekly (excerpts taken from the *Manchester Guardian, Le Monde*, and *The Washington Post*).

New Options (about American grass roots political trends)

New Scientist (British publication that reports on "fringe" but noteworthy technology before it reaches the mainstream)

Release 1.0 (insider newsletter on the computer industry)

The New York Times (daily, Sunday, or Tuesday for the science section)

The Red Herring (monthly magazine on technology startups and offerings, based in Silicon Valley and well-connected with the computer and venture capital powers that be and will be.)

The Wall Street Journal (National, European or Asia editions)

Technology Review (published at M.I.T.; pinpoints cultural implications of new technology)

Wired (read about the social and political ramifications of the computer and tele-communications revolution; see the advertisements that supposedly reflect the tastes and social mores of Generation X)

World Press Review (good review of both news and opinions in a fairly wide array of non-U.S. news periodicals)

On-line and Internet Offerings:

Electronic in-boxes: Netscape, Individual, Bacon's, The Mining Co., and Northern Light are just a few of several for-pay electronic clipping service offerings on the Internet that will scan anywhere from a dozen to several hundred electronic information services daily or weekly, based on your personally-tailored information wish list profile. They deposit the results in your personal electronic in-box. You can then search the results, using key words.

The sources scanned include Reuters, Associated Press, CNN, Business Wire, PR Wire, SIMBA, a long list of special-topic trade publications, and, in some cases, fairly expensive research reports from well-respected research/consulting organizations such as Frost and Sullivan and Veronis, Suhler and Associates that can be downloaded on a page or chapter basis at a pro-rated price. This is a good deal for the aspiring entrepreneur with limited resources, even though some of the reports may be a year or so old.

Most Internet providers, as well as America Online/CompuServe and Prodigy, also offer customers some type of basic complimentary electronic in-box service, but be aware that these services tend to be fairly superficial compared to what is available from the for-pay services. Given these limitations, if you're determined to use one of the major on-line services, CompuServe, now part of America Online, is usually better suited for business research than the others. CompuServe seems to have the best business and technology research sources available, thanks to content agreements that the company was pursuing and nurturing for years before its competitors were even business plans.

At this writing, the Internet provider Netcom had one of the best deals on electronic in-boxes, thanks to a joint offering with Individual, Inc., which also has an independent clipping service for-pay on the World Wide Web. Netcom gives its subscribers Individual's basic service for free.

Netcom and Individual users fill out a basic profile of interests, then receive headlines on up to 20 articles by e-mail each weekday morning. If a user wants to read a complete article, they cut and paste the Internet code from the e-mail message into a Web browser, download it and print it out. Some of the articles are free, some are available for an additional fee. The user receives a daily clipping list of what is available, then can pick and choose. It's the true realization of the daily electronic news service for an audience of one, much talked about in the on-line and media industries for the past decade.

Electronic Newspapers and Magazines:

http://www.hotwired.com — The weekly on-line version of *Wired* magazine, free.

http://www.wsj.com — The on-line daily edition of *The Wall Street Journal*, with major stories from the Asia and Europe editions, for pay.

http://www.nytimes.com/yr/mo/day — Daily editions of *The New York Times*, some sections, free as of fall 1998.

http://www.msnbc.com — New consumer on-line service which complements the new cable TV channel, the progeny of a joint venture between NBC and Microsoft, free.

http://www.nationalreview.com — *The National Review*'s on-line edition. The cyber version of the venerable political journal founded by William F. Buckley, this Web site offers conservative mainstream political thought and commentary, ranging from the advisability of legalizing drugs to privatization of government.

http://www.slate.com/cover — *Slate*, a weekly on-line mainstream political magazine edited by Michael Kinsey, formerly editor of *The New Republic*, funded by Microsoft, for pay.

http://www.upside.com — *Upside*, which also appears in print, is a blend of Forbes-style reportage and *Wired*-style technology previews, free.

http://www.economist.com — The Web edition of *The Economist*, free to those who subscribe to the print version, charges others. This is the whole shebang, and provides an excellent archive resource for those special Survey sections on countries and industry trends, including the charts and graphs.

http://www.asia-inc.com — *Asia Inc.*, which also appears in a slick print edition, is Hong Kong-based and owned by a Thai publisher. Its schizophrenic coverage varies between explaining business dealings and lecturing on social issues, but it accurately reflects the moods of the region. Excellent profiles of Asia power brokers.

Other Electronic Trend Indicators on the Internet:

http://www.futurenet.co.uk/FutureNet — This is a true electronic magazine ("zine," for on-line novices) that offers news, sports, gossip on the Royals, chat links, and very well-connected technology reporting.

http://www.newscientist.com/Planet Science — The Internet version of *New Scientist*, listed above in Periodicals. Smart, leading edge and witty. Perhaps the premier source for technology developments and meaningful explanations for European Internet surfers. Does interviews, answers whacky science questions, and publishes ideas for experiments that might not have worked quite right, or have never been tried.

http://www.townhall.com/Town Hall — This is the on-line Conservative heaven. A highly accessible and active way-station for all things of the U.S. Conservative movement, including the Heritage Foundation, National Review, Americans for Tax Reform and others. Listings, job opportunities, legislative and reference material. Updated daily.

http://www.crpc.rice.edu/CRPC/knowledge-trans/
National Science Foundation — Technology research
and transfer grant announcements. A good
indication of the U.S. government's direction in
funding new technology that may be commercially
viable.

http://www.amazon.com/Amazon.com — Billed as
earth's biggest bookstore, this Internet site not only
lets you buy best-sellers at discount prices by priority
mail, but also features best seller lists in numerous
categories, interviews with authors, reviews by
readers, synopses from *The New York Times Book
Review*, and links to on-line sources about subjects
and authors. Users can read about what's trendy,
then order the book instantly.

http://www.bookwire.com/Publishers Weekly — Get
last week's listings of the top selling fiction, and non-
fiction books, based on sales reports by booksellers
throughout the U.S., plus regular reports on book
categories such as business and self-help titles. All
are linked to amazon.com (above), so two-to-three
day instant gratification is just a click away.

Try out these recommendations on a gradual basis
over two or three months. Add a few favorite sources
of your own, but remember that the objective here is to
tap new resources that you previously have missed. If
possible, build a computer database, including computer
files you can save from the Internet and other on-line
services, plus printed material that can be optically
scanned into the database.

Scan for "The Hunch"

Scan for disconnections, gaps, unserved needs,
barriers that can be reanalyzed, new combinations...let
your mind roll on. Nothing is sacred, there are no

boundaries. Input data from forecasts, models, and information from such sources as the World Future Society and other futurist organizations. These resources can provide the raw material to buttress the entrepreneur's most important tool: informed intuition, more commonly known as "the hunch."

Miyamoto Musashi, the author of *A Book of Five Rings* and a 17th century Japanese samurai, emphasized rational, careful understanding of one's adversaries and the battlefield. However, two of his nine principles of strategy are, "develop intuitive judgement and understanding of everything," and "perceive those things which cannot be seen."[41]

For Musashi as well as modern-day samurai, there's great respect for learning how to form the hunch. And today's samurai knows how to scan.

The types and uses of scanning are limited only by your imagination; ambient scanning, or the technique of reviewing the immediate information and images you come across in a normal day, can stem from reading books or simply observing your environment. It can be the core of new business ideas, and it can become a sort of curiosity game and just plain fun.

Regardless, it is an extremely effective means to begin the Free Market Fusion process.

An interview with Andrew P. Garvin

Garvin is President of Find/SVP, and author of *The Art of Being Well Informed.*

What's your favorite magazine for leisure?

Garvin: *Salt Water Sportsman* or *New York Magazine*

What's your favorite magazine for business?

Garvin: *Forbes*

What's your personal favorite business data source?

Garvin: I'd have to say Dun & Bradstreet, because it remains one of the few sources for information on privately-held companies.

If you were to recommend one best source (printed or electronic) of reliable business research for entrepreneurs preparing a business plan in this climate of increasing uncertainty, what would it be?

Garvin: I'll try to answer the question taking it somewhat literally...i.e., the best source for entrepreneurs preparing a business plan. I don't think there is a single best source. First I'd look at books on the subject, and to get a list of those I'd go to www.amazon.com. Then I'd look for good, solid business articles on the subject and for that I'd go to www.umi.com/proquest or to www.nsearch.com. The latter is a good Web search engine that includes articles available for a small fee. The best source of all might be

the Small Business Administration. See their Web site at
www.sbaonline.sba.gov

**Can an electronic filter truly replace a person's eye
and motivation to know?**

Garvin: Not really. An electronic filter can only
provide information from whatever sources it filters
from. No filter culls from all possible sources that a
trained human could think of to check. Also, it can only
filter what it is asked to filter. Many people are unable
to formulate the right question that will solve their
concern/problem without expert assistance. In other
words, if you ask the wrong question, you're likely to get
the wrong answer.

**How can a business search process be developed
that takes into account what you don't know at all —
outside the box information important for long-range
planning, and enterprise development that isn't
accessible by key words and accepted research
parameters — without having the source list implode?**

Garvin: The only answer I can give to this question
is that such a search process must include input by an
expert professional who has the training, background,
and most of all — experience — to provide the "outside
the box" view.

**How can an individual gauge or measure
information as to its relative importance, in the
increasing chaos of today's environment? Can**

you recommend a more effective technique of benchmarking information?

Garvin: The technique you describe is fine, but lacks one key ingredient — the quality of the source. Any information you get is really only as good as the source it comes from, so the reliability and credibility of the source is critical. In the case of Dun & Bradstreet, for example, much of their information about small privately held companies comes from interviewing the principals of the companies themselves. The information is therefore subject to some question. Nonetheless, it's usually the only thing available, so it's important to know something about how it is gathered.

You provided ample warning in your book about the validity of some Internet sources. My observation is that over the past 18 months or so, many of the mainstream publishing industry's Web sites have matured into highly reliable, breaking news and data sites. Meanwhile, the proliferation of puff and junk sites has mushroomed. Can you recommend some new directories or filters that will take the business researcher or budding entrepreneur doing research on a limited budget to these top sites — and not just the most popular ones?

Garvin: I have yet to try a search engine that really points you ONLY to "top" sites and not just the most popular ones, or the ones the search engines have access to; or the ones some "editor" decides are "good." Some search engines are beginning to integrate "paid" content from presumably established sources (as opposed to just Web sites), but even these are adding this content based upon what deals they can make to get that content. Of course, given enough time spent searching on the Web, one probably can get down to a source that appears reliable, but that takes a lot of time…and who has time these days? My advice is: if you can't find a solid, reliable answer on the Internet in less than 15 minutes, you're probably better off outsourcing it to a professional researcher.

Besides Internet site growth, what is the biggest challenge facing business information researchers over the next five years?

Garvin: The biggest challenge facing business information researchers is to understand that their role is not simply to find information or answer questions. Their role is to understand a client's need and provide a solution within the client's budget. The information itself has become almost a commodity. What counts is the service, consultation, background, and advice that the researcher can provide.

CHAPTER 7

FREE MARKET FUSION TOOLS: SCENARIO BUILDING

Scenario building is an eclectic mix of research, analysis, scientific projection, guess work and hunches.

It is one of those "curious" management practices that is highly regarded in some quarters, and often discounted and impugned in others.

In the words of scenario consulting guru and author Peter Schwartz, president of the Global Business Network, "Scenarios are a tool for helping us to take a long view in a world of great uncertainty...Scenarios are stories about the way the world might turn out tomorrow, stories that can help us recognize and adapt to changing aspects of our present environment. They form a method for articulating the different pathways that might exist for you tomorrow, and finding your appropriate movements down each of those possible paths."[42]

The main purpose of this chapter is to advise the novice on long-term planning. It also provides guidance which will prove useful when selecting a consulting service for scenario building training.

After reading this chapter, you will have a general understanding of the process of scenario building, examples of how it has been employed in certain industries and business opportunity settings, and some references for continued reading and study.

In other words, you will have taken a big step toward perfecting what I call "the art of the hunch."

I'll state my own prejudice right up front: I believe in the practice of scenario building. Properly planned and executed, it is one of the most productive and worthwhile exercises organizations and individuals can undertake. For those who want to identify future Free Market Fusion possibilities, scenario building is essential.

A Game Strategy

Scenarios are part of successful business game strategies, and it is helpful to think of your business as a game played out on the global economy board. Learning scenarios will not only help you prepare for the future, it also will help you actually shape the particular game your business plays, rather than just becoming a participant in someone else's game.[43]

Having stated my prejudice, I also need to offer some caveats. Scenario building should not be treated as fantasy-spinning. To be effective, it takes good, intensive research and data gathering skills, complemented with an interest in history and in social and cultural psychology.

There are a number of good guide books for novices in this craft, including *The Art of the Long View*, by Peter Schwartz; *On Learning to Plan — and Planning to Learn*, by Donald N. Michael, *Conquering Uncertainty*, by Theodore Modis, *Shadow Dancing in the USA*, by

J.P. Tarcher, and, one of the books that truly defined this as a methodology back in the early 1960s, *On Thermonuclear War: Thinking About the Unthinkable*, by the late Herman Kahn, the "dean" of the academic future researchers while he was alive.

In addition, there are many professional journal and magazine articles written on the topic by a wide range of experts and practitioners. *Long Range Planning, Planning Review, Strategy & Business, Harvard Business Review,* and *Sloan Management Review* are good periodical sources for those articles.

Knowing what's good and where to spend your time is important, but perhaps the most important guideline to recognize is to watch out for charlatans posing as scenario building consulting experts.

This field has attracted some truly excellent consulting firms, but it also has attracted its share of "shake-and-bake" experts who will charge hefty fees to work for your company, put you through a forgettable weekend scenario seminar, and not enrich your planning expertise or arsenal one whit.

I am not a full-time practitioner of scenario planning, but have found it to be extremely helpful as part of the Free Market Fusion tool kit. It should be pursued in tandem with other business strategizing and research tools and activities.

Scenarios are No Substitute for Other Planning

One more bit of advice: scenarios are not a "cheap" substitute for other forms of corporate planning, nor should they be considered as islands unto themselves. If they are, they will quickly erode and sink. Scenarios require a considerable investment of management time and effort, and that undoubtedly means a commitment of budget dollars. If they are not valuable and complementary to the other elements of strategic planning, they will surely fail.

In some organizations, as much time is spent marketing the scenarios internally to senior and line management as developing and writing the scenarios themselves. That marketing is every bit as sophisticated as outside marketing programs, and often it takes years to build trust and establish scenario use among managers.

First, some history of scenarios as a management art is instructive.

Wars, Rumors of Wars and the Origins of Scenario Building

You undoubtedly guessed it. Use of scenario building for strategic planning can most directly be traced to the military. But it goes back further than the 1950s-nuclear holocaust-Dr. Strangelove era that many popular books and futurist speakers tend to credit with the seminal beginnings of the scenario craft. Quite a bit further, in fact.

According to Nobel-prize-winning physicist and author Stephen Hawking, in the days of ancient Greece, Rome and Persia, foretelling the future (the arguable objective of the scenario building craft) was the job of oracles or sybils. These were more often than not women who would be drugged or persuaded to breathe fumes from volcanic vents by a group of priests, who would then "interpret" the rantings. It wasn't hard to find someone who would speak unintelligibly under such conditions, so the real market demand was for the interpretations provided by the priests.

The Oracle at Delphi was somewhat notorious for hedging its bets or being ambiguous. Asked by the Spartans what would happen when the Persians attacked, the Oracle said, "Either Sparta will be destroyed, or its king will be killed." Knowing the might of Persia, the priests may well have been scheming that if neither happened, everyone would be so happy and relieved they would forget about the Oracle's prophecy. To everyone's surprise, the king was killed defending the pass at Thermopylae, a battle that saved Sparta and ultimately led to the defeat of the Persian army, guaranteeing a place in posterity for the Oracle.[44] Not bad for breathing some funny-smelling gas.

The Cold War and Futurists

Let's jump ahead to the second half of the 20th century, and the Cold War between the U.S. and the Soviet Union. It was during this era that the development and application of what we today call scenario planning truly emerged. This modern era also has seen the emergence of a new class of popular business and social prophets called futurists. The post-World War II political and military climates provided the seeds of the futurists' rise, as I'll explain.

The use of the war gaming terminology was discouraged in the U.S. military establishment in the 1970s and 1980s, due to the sudden public fascination with such strategy games as Dungeons and Dragons and the popular movie *War Games*. In the film, a teenage hacker inadvertently blunders online into a Defense Department computer that controls nuclear missiles, almost launching World War III.

Because of this sudden surge in popularity, military officials became even more reticent about their own gaming activities and tried to distance themselves from such popular culture phenomena. However, there is reason to believe those phenomena were at least influenced by, and in many cases directly modeled after, military gaming.

Virtually every major business school has adopted some form of scenario building or gaming into its curriculum, as have many executive seminar courses. Corporations have followed suit, with 68 percent of large organizations using some form of scenario planning as of 1983. Though the definitions of the terms vary greatly, it is generally understood that gaming applies just to historical or present-day enactments relying on real-world assessments and data of military or business and economic situations. Scenario building goes a step further and takes a look at the future, anywhere from 6 months to 30 years from the present.

The Rand Corporation

While the Rand Corporation didn't invent scenario development and gaming, it borrowed the idea from military strategists and sold it back to them quite successfully.

The field of technological forecasting evolved near the end of World War II when Allied planners were engaged in round-the-clock projections regarding Germany's actual progress and *possible* theoretical technological advances in building an atomic bomb.

During the 1950s, RAND Corporation's "deep thinkers" analyzed the relationship between weapons development and military strategy. Within the military-industrial network, Herman Kahn and a close group of associates turned their analytical skills to scenario building. Also at RAND during this time, but working separately, the mathematician Olaf Helmer proposed a theoretical basis for using expert opinion in forecasting, the foundation of what is today known as the Delphi methodology.

Kahn used his own scenario techniques as part of the basis of *On Thermonuclear War*, which examined the possible consequences of nuclear war. Supposedly, the book also made Kahn the archetype for the role of the somewhat deranged scientist in the popular doomsday comedy movie, *Dr. Strangelove*. Kahn, who may have been emphatic but was anything but deranged, recovered from his association with the movie character. He went on to found the Hudson Institute, and devoted many of his remaining years to applying classical conservative economic theories to world growth projections.

Game playing by Russian military strategists has become better understood since the collapse of the Soviet Union and the more open discussions and information sharing between Western and Russian military gamers. Ironically, most Russian game playing during the Cold War centered around a massive ground war in Europe, as did that of NATO. On both sides, game situations usually included a hypothetical response to the other side suddenly introducing tactical nuclear weapons into the supposed conflict. But never did game tacticians admit to proposing a pre-emptive nuclear strike by their own side.

Game-playing scenarios, usually with strong secrecy, continue to be a favorite planning tool within organizations like the Naval War College, Army War College, Air University, National Defense University, and the Industrial College of the Armed Forces.

While the military was financing think-tank research into gaming, there was considerable parallel development leading to scenario exercises in the civilian world. In 1964 the French social scientist Bertrand de Jouvenel published *L'Art de la conjecture*, which offered a systematic rationale for the field of futurology. According to David Mercer, former head of the Centre for

Strategy and Policy at the Open University School of Management, London, the concept also was introduced by G. Berger in *La Prospective*, in 1964. Herman Kahn is credited with first using the word "scenario" in a forecasting context in 1967.[45] Mercer maintains that the true theoretical foundations of scenario forecasting were developed between 1974 and 1979 by M. Godet, as explained in Godet's book, *Scenarios and Strategic Management* (1987).[46, 47]

Scenarios and Global Growth

In 1972, *The Limits to Growth* was published by the Club of Rome, an informal association of about 70 members of 25 nationalities including scientists, educators, economists, humanists and industrialists. The book presented some of the first truly data-based projections on the consequences of global population growth. It used a computer model, research and a report prepared by a team of MIT researchers led by postgraduate students Dennis and Dana Meadows and headed by Jay W. Forrester. The team's work was funded by a $240,000 grant from the Volkswagen Foundation.[48]

Forrester was a one-time professor of computer engineering who had done break-through computer systems and software design before moving over to take a position at what is now MIT's Sloan School of Management.

The Limits to Growth was widely publicized by the news media as a global wakeup call. But it spurred a controversial response from another researcher,

Cesare Marchetti, a physicist at the International Institute of Advanced Systems Analysis near Vienna, Austria. Using the S-curve, a variant of bell curve prediction theories, Marchetti believed that fundamental laws which govern growth and competition among species may also describe human activities, and that competition among species and within human activities would lead to equilibrium.

The growth curves he calculated in response to the Club of Rome hypothesis predicted that it was possible to sustain a human population of 1 trillion on earth without exhausting any primary resource, including the environment. This argument branded Marchetti as a reactionary maverick among his scientific peers, but placed him in familiar company with other iconoclastic futurists of the era.[49]

According to Swiss author and physicist Theodore Modis, who interviewed Marchetti at length in the mid-1980s for his own book, Marchetti was dogmatic, at times arrogant, and extremely persuasive when he explained his calculations.[50] Modis' discussions with the Austrian physicist and related inquiries led him to a shift in careers from strategic planning for a large computer firm to full-time research and writing on the theory and applications of S-curves. Modis' most recent book explaining the applications of S-curve theories to businesses, *Conquering Uncertainty*, was published in early 1998 (see the interview at the end of this chapter).

By the early 1980s, scenario forecasting had become highly sophisticated, and was used primarily to integrate the output from other sophisticated approaches to long-range planning. Scenario forecasting was based upon judgmental forecasts, according to Mercer, and its various techniques most commonly centered around bringing together groups of experts in order to reduce the risk of being completely wrong. The techniques used included Delphi Methodology and cross-impact matrices, which appeared impressive because they could reflect data and a huge range of possibilities. But they were expensive and usually demanded the resources of a central planning staff.

Royal Dutch Shell: a Scenario Success

So, why the acceptance by corporations of such a seemingly inexact and often expensive planning approach?

In a nutshell, because the alternative was even worse. This was demonstrated by the 1973 Arab-Israel War and the Oil Shock that followed. Though other examples undoubtedly exist, the popular favorite case is Royal Dutch Shell, one of the first companies to get it right. Shell had initiated scenario development to guide its long-term strategy in 1971, under the guidance of Pierre Wack.[51]

Though Shell took its lumps in the 1973 Oil Shock and aftermath, its corporate planners are generally credited with having been the only group of major oil company managers to have "thought outside the box" of conventional opinion and considered what they might do if the era of cheap Middle Eastern oil suddenly came to an end.

As a result, when the Arab oil embargo and resulting price increases went into effect, Shell management was already familiar with a list of possible responses. These did not include operational plans ready to be deployed at a moment's notice, but in the minds of Shell managers, they at least were not caught flat-footed. On an intellectual awareness and emotional preparedness level, Shell was ready to take action. Development of North Sea oil drilling was accelerated; other non-Middle East reserves were plumbed, and pricing structures were put into effect that allowed Shell to climb over the backs of some of its competitors.

The results were dramatic, thanks in no small part to the fact that Wack had been preaching his scenarios within Shell for months before the crisis. Over the next few years during the crisis, Shell rose from the bottom ranks of the world's big oil companies to become one of the two largest and, arguably, the most profitable, according to Peter Schwartz, who consulted for Wack in the late 1970s. Schwartz eventually replaced Wack when he retired from Shell in 1982.[52]

There are numerous other examples of companies who got it right, got it wrong, and then got it right again. These include IBM, AT&T, Apple, Sony, Honda, Microsoft, Intel, and Turner Broadcasting.

A Scenario for Federal Express

In a recent "hypothetical" scenario development seminar led by Coates & Jarrett, a Washington, D.C.-based planning consulting firm, one of my associates helped cast a scenario based on the question, "Should Federal Express develop an open information bidding system in which shippers place transport services orders, and carriers, including competitors to Federal Express, bid in real-time for these jobs?"

To help FedEx make up its mind, the seminar participants were asked to draw up four scenarios describing the world of 2025 and how FedEx or its successor organizations might appear. Four groups of scenario developers were given four different contexts with which to develop their scenarios.

The scenarios varied from the apocalyptic to the sanitized. What was most striking about them was that all described a world in which FedEx was in the information management business, with physical delivery services ranging from a secondary role to part of its recent past.

Oh, and by the way, FedEx announced its shift to an open information system a few weeks after the seminar.

Picking the Right Kind of Scenario Planning

So, to answer the obvious question, do all of these companies use some form of scenario planning? Yes.

What kind? It varies, and most companies constantly mix the planning tools they use.

Again, my objective in this chapter is to give a rudimentary background that will assist the reader in appreciating the value of scenario planning, as well as to give pointers on what to look for when deciding what form of scenario planning will be most beneficial.

For a chart which presents some — but certainly not all — of the most prevalent scenario planning methods, see Table A at the end of the chapter. I've assembled it from the work and published recommendations of some of the top consultants in the field, as well as my own experience and that of some of my associates.

From the Horses' Mouths: Views of Scenario Gurus

The best type of scenario planning is the one that stimulates you and your colleagues to informed, spirited, management discussion and, eventually, decisions. Some methods are loose and informal, others are highly structured and fact-based. This is a case where the personality of the scenario method should fit the character of the participants in the scenario process.

Here are the views of three distinctly different scenario design consultants who head up very successful consulting practices aiding companies and organizations in scenario design:

David Mason, Northeast Consulting Resources, Inc., Boston, Mass.: "The collaborative, pragmatic discipline of Future Mapping pinpoints key issues even when divisive opinions exist. By sharpening the focus on industry specifics, it draws actionable chunks of information from the group. The organization gains the ability to learn (and unlearn) faster, to forecast better, and to chart a course, as a proactive participant, towards a desired future.

"For planners, Future Mapping also serves as a periscope for checking on the validity of the scenarios as time goes by. By being aware of the mileposts and direction signs that mark each path, you can adjust strategy as the future unfolds. This is an extremely powerful idea, the key to shifting an organization's focus from analysis to action."

Peter Schwartz, Global Business Network, Emeryville, Calif.: "Driving forces often seem obvious to one person and hidden to another. That is why I almost always compose scenarios in teams...After identifying and exploring the 'driving forces,' one must uncover the 'predetermined elements' and the 'critical uncertainties.' Some scenario builders — including Pierre Wack — refuse to give definitions for any elements at all. They believe that any definition would trivialize the subtleties of the process. Scenario creation is not a reductionist process; it is an art, as is story-telling."[53]

Joseph F. Coates, Coates & Jarrett, Inc., Washington, D.C.: "Scenarios are written for the organization that will use them. There is not much sense in using scenarios written for the Environmental Protection Agency in strategy-making for the Department of Labor, because the two agencies have different missions and are quite naturally interested in different parts of the world. (This runs contrary to the ideal that every agency should be interested in looking at everything. You have to be practical and recognize that scenarios stretch an already limited span of surveillance.)"[54]

In the words of Lawrence Wilkinson, writing in a special edition of *Wired* magazine entitled *Wired Scenarios*, the relevance of scenario exercises is hard to refute: "Scenario planning derives from the observation that, given the impossibility of knowing precisely how the future will play out, a good decision or strategy to adopt is one that plays out well across several possible futures."[55] Hence, the need for more than one scenario in any exercise, not to mention getting more value for your buck from the scenario consultants who lead you through it.

There is no one right way to conduct scenario planning, though there are a few approaches that are so simplistic as to have little long-term value. What follows is a summary description that I have dubbed "The 7 Steps of Scenario Planning" in keeping with the current popular formula for management advice. This is a synthesis of many methods that are presently used and in which I or my colleagues have participated, and I don't pretend that they are original; I've tried to give credit where credit is due throughout this chapter.

Following "The 7 Steps" is a case study of one scenario building exercise that my company had the opportunity to be part of in late 1996 concerning the future of the computer industry. I urge anyone considering scenario building to review these options and experiences, read the prevailing literature cited here and in other sources, and then embark on some scenario training courses before applying it to their companies or using it as a technique to define scenarios for business opportunities.

The 7 Steps of Scenario Planning

Step 1: Recruiting Senior Management

Unless you already run your own business or other organization, the most crucial step is to make your boss — preferably the head of the company — a believer in scenario building. If you're several levels down in the hierarchy, find out who is in charge of strategic planning, meet them, and volunteer to be a participant, guinea pig, or volunteer gofer in preparing for strategy planning sessions or, hopefully, scenario exercises. If the company already uses them, you may quickly be pinpointed as a "resource." If it does not, then you'll be in position to campaign for using scenario development in the future. Become a missionary, advocating long-term planning.

Step 2: Posing the Question

Almost every scenario leads from a "What if?" question relating to the company's future or its industry's future, and it's almost impossible to build a scenario without one. Examples might include:

"Should we divest our land-land technology and invest only in satellite and wireless?";

"What if trade war breaks out with Asia and high tariffs are levied on all overseas products?";

"What if satellite transmissions are interrupted for several months world-wide?";

"How should our company be prepared to respond to the consumer market in Africa if AIDs treatments successfully stem the disease by the year 2005?"

Posing such questions yields the facts and data needed to begin to assemble the parameters for a company or social environment in the future.

Step 3: Environmental Analysis and Fact Gathering: aka Defining Driving Forces

Here's where the scanning techniques and disciplines discussed in Chapter 6 come into play. Depending on how many participants there are in this exercise, you'll need anywhere from several dozen to several hundred sets of events and facts — real ones, not hypothetical. These will be used to assign descriptions around several key parameters that are in turn linked to the question driving this exercise.

Examples of driving events (events which are influential but certain to change) are:

- China's average education level is 10th-grade;

- Per barrel price of oil increase stays below world-wide inflation.

Examples of facts likely to change over a long period of time (or never) are:

- Moore's law of computing power remains true;

- UN and Western countries finance AIDs treatment to eradicate the disease in Africa.

These are positive examples, but there should be plenty of negative ones, as well. The idea is that the facts will support and dictate the parameters, also known as driving forces.

Step 4: Driving Forces

Global Business Network categorizes most of its driving forces into four groups: *Social dynamics* (such as demographics), *economic issues* (such as what are competitors likely to do), *political issues* (such as who will be President), and *technological issues* (such as agreements on wireless bandwidth). Other practitioners have similar groupings. If no facts are available for one of these areas, the researchers must be sent back to their databases and files before the driving forces can be properly defined.

Step 5: Setting Up A Matrix

The scenario development team usually sets up an axis (see Figure 6) to which the driving forces can be assigned. The matrix represents extremes in the future environment, such as a *laissez faire* world business environment vs. trade wars and regulation, or cheap technology/wired citizenry vs. technology haves/majority have nots. The driving forces and their supporting facts are then clustered into the matrix quadrants. If the scenario group is large enough to assign responsibility for each quadrant to sub-groups, separate writing exercises begin. In a smaller group, the whole team may write all the scenarios, which is challenging.

Figure 6 is an example based on the following hypothetical situation: an entrepreneur with experience in both the computer and oil and gas industries is to advise a major university in a middle-eastern country whether it should invest in establishing a new department for educating technology professionals in the application of western-produced computerized monitoring and research instruments for the oil and gas industry.

To gather information for the final recommendation, the entrepreneur staged a scenario workshop of a dozen computer and oil and gas consultants, analysts, and economists. The workshop was divided into four teams, each charged with writing a scenario based on the four general sets of conditions in the Figure 6 matrix. Each was asked to postulate on demand for technology professionals, based on the scenario.

Figure 6

Scenario Development Matrix

Key Question: Should a middle-eastern university invest in establishing a new department dealing with conventional oil and gas technology monitoring?

Vertical axis: technology availability

Horizontal axis: trade and business environment

Cheap technology	
Scenario A	Scenario B
*Caspian Sea oil boom	*Asian republics join OPEC
*Russia democratizes	*China & Japan form trade block
*Iraq coup; embargo lifted	*Mexico adopts dollar
Laissez faire ————————	———— Trade wars
Scenario C	Scenario D
*Latin America floats currencies	*Japan embargoes U.S. electronics
*oil shortage	*OPEC hikes oil tariffs
*move to hydrogen fuel	*U.S. nullifies NAFTA
Expensive technology	

Step 6: Writing Scenarios

Looking at where the forces and facts have clustered, the scenario team writes a description of how the business or other environment will appear next to the primary question, with four or more different scenarios. Additional scenarios can come from subdividing the quadrants, and this can become especially interesting if different teams are asked to describe the environment with slightly different sets of driving forces. However, it is usually best to consolidate down to three or four scenarios for the final outcome.

As an example, the four scenarios produced from the Scenario Development Matrix (Figure 6) that appears on page 151 are summarized as follows:

Scenario A: Laissez Faire Economics and Cheap Technology

Trade barriers fall and free market policies take the lead in Central Asia, allowing plentiful Caspian Sea oil to reach the world's markets. Positive trade balances and new revenues lead to the importation of new technology from the West into much of Asia, and the development of consumer technology markets. Meanwhile, Russia enters a period of true democratization in a post-Yeltsen era, stabilizing that country's economic system and government. In the Persian Gulf, Iraqi President Saddam Hussein is overthrown in a coup, and is replaced by a military government that agrees to disarm and set up a schedule for moving that country toward democratic elections and government. The overall stability and promise bring new investment to all three regions and set the stage for a promising era of economic development and progress.

Outcome: There is rapid growth in demand for energy industry technology professionals.

Scenario B: Trade wars and cheap technology

Trade barriers remain a constant as Asian republics join with OPEC to form a more powerful trading block. This is enhanced by the agreement of Western oil companies to help these developing countries with oil production and transportation, despite anti-West trade policies. China and Japan, partly in defense and partly in retaliation, form a Sino-Japanese trading block aimed at encouraging the new OPEC group to give these two countries preferential treatment with trade tariffs. Meanwhile, Mexico drops the peso in favor of the dollar as its currency, and joins with the U.S. and Canada to become the suppliers of technology to the rest of Latin America.

Outcome: New demand for technology training, but difficulty recruiting some new faculty from the West.

Scenario C: Laissez faire and expensive technology

Most Latin American countries float their currencies, making them more dependent than ever on their dollar reserves and in need of U.S. imports, which the U.S. is quick to supply almost tariff-free. But a world-wide shortage in oil supplies keeps technology expensive.

Development of hydrogen fuel technologies as a replacement for carbon fuel transportation and industrial power will upset the balance of power among oil-rich states. However, this is partly mitigated by major oil companies looking to expand and stabilize their asset bases by underwriting much of the hydrogen fuel research. Market barriers for all types of technology are kept low as countries such as China, Saudi Arabia, and Russia strive to acquire technology and professional work forces that can exploit new technologies.

Outcome: Short-term demand for new training and professionals in conventional oil production. Long-term is uncertain.

Scenario D: Expensive technology and trade wars

This is the least optimistic scenario. Japan, outraged at the U.S.'s continued pressure to reform its banking sector, retaliates by hiking tariffs on a wide range of U.S. products. This leads to an all-out trade war between North America and Asia, the latter having only partially recovered from the 1997-98 financial collapse. OPEC leaps into the fray by hiking oil prices in an attempt to break the U.S.-British political hammerlock on Gulf politics. Faced with a deteriorating economic situation in Mexico and South America, the U.S. Congress nullifies NAFTA and imposes tight border controls with Mexico. The world appears to be entering a period of isolationism among nations. A bright point is the offer by U.S. and German banks to guarantee continued loan supports to developing countries in return for more free market-oriented policies.

Outcome: Demand for new technology training is limited. Middle-east oil producers look for professionals experienced in "old" technology and retrofitting.

Step 7: Identifying Issues and Tailoring Strategies

Each team writes and then presents its scenario to the other sections of the team. Teams offer rationale, argue and defend. This can be a high-spirited, fun debate. Each team then, ideally, writes up a set of corporate strategies to help contend with the hypothetical scenario, and further explains them to upper management. The end result: everyone has an opportunity to try "out of the box" thinking and to look at possible combinations of events and driving forces that may never before have been considered. When one or more of these events does occur in the future, perhaps in a still more different scenario, the managers may have strategies or parts of strategies in mind that seem familiar and plausible. This works very well for the individual, as well. Placing yourself in the future, then working backwards, can be a valuable skill in dealing with an uncertain world.

One demonstration of a scenario building process my company joined is explained in detail in Appendix B. There are many more, and an especially good resource for recent scenarios is the World Wide Web, where consulting firms often post the results of scenario building exercises for a variety of clients who agree to the public release of the information. Besides the sources cited here and in the chapter's end notes, a simple search using any of the standard Internet search engines will turn up a wealth of resources and examples. Build your own scenario process, one that works for you.

The scenario process is a perfect example of what this book is all about, perfecting the art of the hunch.

Welcome and good luck in the new era of Free Market Fusion.

An Interview with Theodore Modis

Physicist and author of *Predictions* (1992) and *Conquering Uncertainty* (1998)

How does the Asia financial markets crisis beginning in the fall of 1997 stack up against the stock market crash of 1987 in predictability, especially using the historical 56-year S-curves you advocate in your first book *Predictions*?

Modis: Please understand that you can't develop a hypothesis, then look for individual events with which to build an S-curve. However, just doing a superficial look, if the fall of 1997's events follow the approximate 56 year cycle on a regional basis (not global), it would coincide with 1941, when European colonial economic rule in Asia essentially came to an end with the invasion of those Asia colonies by Japan, necessitating the evolution of different economic systems.

There are also technology events that may coincide, such as 1885, when steam replacing sails on ships reached 50 percent saturation and possibly began to come into its own in terms of energy efficiency, and, likewise, air travel beginning to replace steamship travel during WWII.

A similar regional pattern exists which might be traced for the U.S. stock market slide of October, 1987 — about two years late, by my calculations, but within a standard margin of error. By the way, I got tired of holding cash and invested in the market the Friday before Black Monday.

You tag the computer/electronics industries as "old." Yet they may be the primary engines of growth in the developed countries that carry forward the period of economic escalation you predicted. Is it possible they have growth curves that are somewhat different from your predicted 90 percent saturation by 2006?

Modis: Microsoft, for example is in the early summer or late spring of its life, but still on front of the S curve. Late summer is the turning point for any company. Based on the curves, IBM will have a life of 120-150 years, while Digital only had a life of 30 years. [Digital's acquisition by Compaq was announced the week of the interview with Modis]. The turning point is when the rate of growth starts declining. How to identify that point is, of course, the trick.

I think the computer industry overall is still in the early summer stage because mutations are still occurring, such as cheaper and cheaper microprocessors, and more and more miniaturization. This is feeding into the niche demand for mobile intelligent machines, such as lap tops, digital assistants, cell phones, and pagers.

What is the S-curve for the management style and philosophy of entrepreneurship?

Modis: Entrepreneurship is not a part of the summer of an S-curve, because this is when growth is fastest and profit is highest. Entrepreneurship thrives in the winter cycles, when growth is flat or uncertain, and something needs to happen to keep the curve moving. These are difficult economic periods that coincide with new ideas. Excellence and creativity are more appropriate in the winter period. Whenever something is in transition, entrepreneurship thrives.

Concerning the acquisition of entrepreneurial companies by conglomerates — WebTV by Microsoft, for example — is the smaller entrepreneurial company's S-curve obliterated by the new owner?

Modis: It is very complex to plot these companies — in some cases an entrepreneurial company is taken over, but its culture rises to the top; in other cases, it is completely absorbed and subsumed by the bigger company. S-curves really do need to be micro, so in many cases it works better with corporate entities than with an entire industry. This is where predator and prey cycles start playing out, the ratio of foxes to rabbits. Yet, big predators like Microsoft aren't operating because of the free will of Bill Gates — they are there because there is a niche market for their products, and a source to fill that niche would have evolved regardless of what personality was or was not born. What is interesting is which cycle companies are in: summer, winter or second summer. Also, whether they are foxes or rabbits in the predator cycle. Sometimes a big company is known as a fox and acquires a little rabbit company whose CEO has been a fox in disguise all along.

How do you reconcile recognizing a place for entrepreneurship against your repudiation of free will playing a decisive role in corporate growth and performance? Are you saying that Apple Computer

was inevitable, and Microsoft, and Digital Equipment Corp., even if the personalities — or someone similar to them — of Steve Jobs, Bill Gates and Ken Olsen never existed?

Modis: Companies grow like organisms. Lots of conditions have to be there. Then somebody had to put the seed in the ground. A personality can't create the growth potential — but it can plant the seed. Digital with 130,000 employees was way beyond Ken Olsen's ability to control.

Free will cannot make a product live longer. A product can only fill a market niche — the niche may sometimes seem to be created by the product — such as PCs, faxes, modems, cell phones — but, in fact, there was a potential there among a certain number of people who wanted to communicate more effectively, and market forces that compelled them to want to.

You cannot create a need by impressions of advertising, just create an awareness of need and choices.

Additional references for preparing scenario exercises and studies:

Competitive Advantage, by Michael Porter, New York: Free Press, 1985

Conquering Uncertainty, by Theodore Modis, New York: Business Week Books, 1998

The Fifth Discipline, by Peter Senge, New York: Doubleday/Currency, 1990

Six Thinking Hats, by Edward de Bono, Boston: Little, Brown & Co., 1985

Charting the Corporate Mind, by Charles Hampden-Turner, New York: The Free Press, 1990

The Pursuit of Wow!, Tom Peters, New York: Vintage, 1994

Every Street Is Paved With Gold, Kim Woo-Choong, Quilcen, WA: Quill, 1995

The Popcorn Report, Faith Popcorn, New York: Harper, 1992

Paradigms, The Business of Discovering the Future, Joel Arthur Barker, New York: Harper, 1993

Table A
Selection of Scenario and Forecasting Development Models

Type of Approach	Organization	Description	Comments	Resources
I Royal Dutch Shell – Traditional	Various consulting firms	Simulate possible futures to make managers better prepared to react to multiple futures. Spurs debate on possible options and the futures which may require them.	This is the dominant model in strategic planning literature and the one with the greatest depth of history. Looking at Royal Dutch's success, it's hard to argue against it.	Peter Schwartz, *The Art of the Long View*; Pierre Wack, "Uncharted Waters Ahead," *Harvard Business Review*, Sept/Oct 1985, also "Scenarios: Shooting the Rapids," *Harvard Business Review*, Nov/Dec, 1985 Arie de Geus, "Planning as Learning," *Harvard Business Review*, March/April, 1988
II Royal Dutch Shell – Current	Royal Dutch Shell – Many emulators	Includes focused scenarios, links to competitive positioning, strategic vision, and options management, all to ensure actionability and life after creation of the scenarios.	Royal Dutch Shell continues to inspire other organizations and practitioners in scenario work. They are among the innovators in the field.	Paul J.H. Shoemaker and Cornelius A.J.M. van der Heijden, "Integrating Scenarios into Strategic Planning at Royal Dutch/Shell," *Planning Review*, May/June 1992, p. 41-46
BASICS (Battelle Scenario Inputs to Corporate Strategy)	Battelle Institute	Strong orientation toward technology forecasting. Very highly developed approach to driving force scenarios.	Preparation requires use of large set of interlocking techniques and big assumptions about the effects of trends on other trends.	Battelle Institute; also, references to these scenario techniques and many others are related by Stephen M. Millett, and Edward J. Honton in *Manger's Guide to Technology Forecasting and Strategy Analysis Methods*, Battelle Press, 1991
Participant-directed	Global Business Network	An offspring of the traditional Royal Dutch Shell method. Emphasizes scenario plots. Considers scenario writing to be closely similar to the work of a painter or novelist. Important are hopes and fears, dreams, and beliefs. Scenarios are "myths about the future."	Touted, but rather vaguely explained in *The Art of the Long View*	Peter Schwartz, *The Art of the Long View*, New York, Doubleday/Currency,1996; also, see Global Business Network's Web page, http://www.gbn.org/; includes description of scenario building, several articles and white papers, extensive lists of recommended books, and several final scenarios growing out of GBN's work for various clients

Table A (Continued)
Selection of Scenario and Forecasting Development Models

Type of Approach	Organization	Description	Comments	Resources
Future Mapping	Northeast Consulting Resources, Inc.	The basic notion is that planning requires learning and re-perceiving the business environment. The process includes line managers to share organizational learning. Uses "endstates" (future snapshots) and large sets of measurable trigger events from a real-world database.	Future Mapping is a proprietary and complex scenario method. The approach has been used to sort out such thorny issues as the economic future of China, electronic commerce strategies for international banking, and design of new customer interfaces across multiple business units of a Fortune 50 manufacturer.	See Northeast Consulting's Web page, http://www.ncri.com/ Given its attraction to technology-based clients and industries, this group's scenarios tend to be very much near-term
Decision Focus process	SRI International	SRI is the best known proponent of driving force scenarios. Recognizes the need for a culture shift to make scenarios useful in the organization. Considers how to target key opportunities for the use of scenarios in the organization.	Unlike many of the other practitioners who help cast scenarios, then let the chips fall where they may, SRI's process makes explicit efforts to connect scenario views to organizational outcomes.	Ian Wilson, "Teaching Decision Makers to Learn from Scenarios: A Blueprint for Implementation," *Planning Review*, May/June 1992, p.18-23
Strategy via Persuasion Scenarios	Coates & Jarratt, Inc.	Focuses on persuading managers and top executives that there is more than one possible future, through examining facts, particularly technology forecasts, against various possible social, economic, and political trends, then addressing viable strategies for each.	Coates & Jarratt maintain that there is no single predicable future and, in fact, that no two organizations should be expected or encouraged to design the same scenarios. The scenarios should be complex and integrated, and evolved with the thought that strategies to which they are attached must be pragmatic.	Joseph F. Coates, John B. Mahaffie and Andy Hines, *2025: Scenarios of US and Global Society Reshaped by Science and Technology*, Akron, Ohio: Oak Hill Press, 1996

Sources: Coates & Jarratt, Inc.; Global Business Network; NCRI Inc.; Planning Review; Jay S. Mendall, Nonextrapolative Methods in Business Forecasting: Scenarios, Vision and Issues Management, Westport, Conn. and London, England; Quorum Books, 1985.

CHAPTER 8

THE RULES OF THE FREE MARKET FUSION GAME

Many years ago, a favorite game among children in the mining towns of the Allegheny Mountains in the Eastern U.S. involved iron fragments, matching pieces of coal, magnets, and placing bets.

The coal and iron would be mixed together in a bag, then dumped out in three mounds in the center of a sheet of butcher paper that had been suspended about 10 inches off the floor on a simple wood frame. Two opposing six-inch circles were drawn near the borders of the paper.

The two players were each given a small magnetized piece of iron two or three inches long. The object of the game was to see how many iron fragments could be moved out of the mounds and into the circles by sliding the magnets under the sheet. Both the players and the bystanders bet on how many iron fragments a player would move into his circle in a set time, usually about 10 minutes.

Of course, the challenge was that the players were blindfolded after being given 30 seconds to study the playing board and the structure of each mound. The players had to rely on memory, instinct, and the cheers and directions (or mis-directions) of the fans. Their skill progressed rapidly, building quickly on each previous game's experience.

It was a good way to develop the art of the hunch at an early age.

Gathering the right elements together to successfully make it through the Free Market Fusion process need not be so chancy, providing the entrepreneur participant understands the discipline of the process.

There's little time to be wasted on trying to move lumps of coal, or leaving iron fragments on the fringe of the circle in haste. Establishing a disciplined pattern of progress is important, but also important is being sensitive to spot observations of others, and relying on memory, or a knowledge base.

One of the purposes of this book is to help the reader refine the art of the hunch, while at the same time narrowing the field of probabilities that a final decision must be made by any significant degree of guesswork.

I think of the combined skill, experience, and judgement of an entrepreneur and his partners as a magnet. The path taken with the magnet can either follow the main process (Figure 2), or it can leapfrog certain steps. Customarily, it usually must move all of the key elements, such as scanning, a knowledge database, partners, and strategic plans and agreements along generally the same path, to the point where the new enterprise goes into its key action phase. At this stage, new energy is created (fusion), meaning that the mission is successfully fulfilled. Whether and how to continue the partnership then becomes an important question, but the process of assembling the resources, and who among the parties has a strong, or legal sense of ownership, will almost dictate this decision process.

Here are the key rules to be followed:

1. A Free Market Fusion enterprise might only be break-even; be realistic, and realize this may be satisfactory for your partners. Be realistic about your own needs in Stage 1, when you're scanning for opportunities.

2. Gather your data and build your knowledge base while openly exploring the next steps of the process with your potential partners. Be open about the process you expect to go through and solicit their ideas.

3. Don't create sacred cows that bog down the process. Steps such as scenario building, Stage 2 (Chapter 7), can be essential — or completely dispensable.

4. When moving with your partners into Stage 3 (Chapters 2 – 5 and the case studies), the action phase, establish mutually agreeable performance guidelines, including timelines. Decide who is in charge; honor that agreement unless the operation is definitely on the verge of derailing.

5. Throughout the process, consciously pay attention to the importance of imagination and fresh ideas. Be tolerant of them so that they are encouraged even if discarded later.

6. Concentrate on solutions and desired results. Eventually, you must pay attention to conflicts, paradoxes and the like, but if you concentrate on solutions and results, conflicts might get resolved in the process.

7. Recognize when it's over for you, or time to assume a new role. Stage 4 (Chapters 1 and 8), the outcome assessment, is an excellent opportunity to reshape the partnership if the enterprise is to continue.

There are occasional opportunities where a partnership is formed almost spontaneously, the partners assemble the necessary resources, and the mission is accomplished before they even considered doing extensive research, and most certainly not such an elaborate step as scenario planning. Don't worry about it, but don't count on it happening "like magic" more than once or twice in the course of your career.

Developing the habits of good observation and research — all the elements of effective scanning — are two of the most important outcomes of any Free Market Fusion endeavor, regardless of how successful or unsuccessful a particular enterprise becomes. These are skills that will serve the entrepreneur well in any capacity.

In the end, the art of the hunch is perfected through the sum of experience and knowledge gained by the practitioner.

Eventually, the partners may go through the Free Market Fusion process almost by second nature, varying it depending on the new set of elements and mission contingencies.

The final rule is to not let the process dictate the nature of the enterprise; discipline is important, but success often goes to those who recognize the next level or opening of opportunity, and chart an immediate course to reach it.

CHAPTER 9

THE FREE MARKET FUSION INDEX

The Free Market Fusion Index is a self-test to determine the reader's — or an organization's — aptitude for undertaking entrepreneurial ventures in the Free Market Fusion arena. The test is available to take, with immediate results, on the World Wide Web at *freemarketfusion.com*.

This chapter provides a few example questions from the Index, and a few of the outcomes based on test ratings done at the Web site. It is not possible to self-test and compile your own score based on the questions given here, since the questions are weighted differently and are much more detailed in the interactive version.

Fusion Index

Organization:

Rate your organization and yourself as to the likelihood that Free Market Fusion could happen or has happened, and what your standing will be if it does:

Age of organization:

over 20__; 15-20__; 5-15___; 3-5___; 0-3___

Source of capital:

%public___; %private___; don't know (check)_____

Will the primary source of capital shift over the next 24 months?

yes/no

No. of employees: _____

No. of products/services that provide revenues: _____

Do you sell your own branded products/services?

_____ yes _____ no

What is the time to launch a new product or service, from approval date by management? (check one)

under 6 months___; 6 months-12 months___; over 12 months___

Does the organization have a form, paper or electronic, for proposing new ideas?

_____ yes _____ no

Is organizational financial data available to employees preparing proposals?

_____ yes _____ no

Circle the organization's culture:

- participatory/democratic (decisions made by consensus)
- entrepreneurial/democratic (consensus opinion sought before decisions made)
- entrepreneurial/autocratic (employee opinions sought on informal basis)
- autocratic/bureaucratic (top management or owner makes all decisions)

Personal Fusion Index:

Preference for organizational culture:

- democratic
- entrepreneurial
- autocratic

Length of time with the organization?

_____ less than 2 years; _____ 2-5 years; _____ over 5 years

Your position with the company:

_____ top management; _____ middle-level; _____ soldier

Self-perception:

_____ leader; _____ leader and good follower; _____ lone wolf;
_____ strategic team member; _____ tactical implementer

Personal life:

    ____ single; ____ married; ____ children;

    ____ plan to change personal status within 12 months

Education level:

    ___ HS; ___ 2 years college; ___ 4 years college;

    ___ graduate degree; ___ post-graduate work

Volunteer work:

    ___ 10 hours per month; ___ 20 hours per month

    ___ 30 hours per month; ___ Less than 10 hours per month

Years in workforce since completing most recent post high school education:

    ____ Under 2; ____ 2-5; ____ 5-10; ____ over 10

Means of financing own business:

Primarily (over 50%) personal loans ____

Primarily savings ____

Have private backing available (not loans) ____

RFD (combination of relatives, friends and personal debt ____

Has your income ever been totally dependent on sales commissions?

    ____ yes ____ no

On a scale of 100 possible points, your organization Fusion Index is ____ (fill in score here from Web site)

On a scale of 100 possible points, your personal Fusion Index is ____ (fill in score here from Web site)

We recommend you rate both.

Example outcomes of index:

Scores

35

Organization: Possibility of fusion is nil; organization will be disassembled within five years or taken over by another group.

Individual: Consider immediate career change, including new training/education.

58

Organization: Fusion likely to occur, but equally high risk of destruction. Competitive battle for survival, with markets and product flows likely to change entirely within five years. Top management will turn over; over 50% of middle managers will change jobs or be eliminated.

Individual: Survival depends on maximum flexibility and versatility, ability and willingness to take pay cuts, or adapt to new compensation plans, take on undesirable or exceedingly difficult assignments.

91

Organization: Fusion will occur. Will emerge as leader in its field within five years; will demonstrate innovation to its customers and exceedingly high value, as evidenced in its market position and new alliances with former competitors, or with partners new to the industry. Will have demonstrated ability to find new sources of capital or shift its reliance on previous sources.

Individual: Individual understands strategic role-playing and positioning and likes it. Will assume a major leadership position within organization, or launch own entrepreneurial venture; possible recruitment by another organization to a better position.

Appendix A — A Scenario Case Study: Mapping the Future of Computing

In October, 1996, at the invitation of Northeast Consulting Resources Inc. (NCRI) and *Communications Week* magazine, Jones International had the chance to participate in a scenario building exercise with 50 other business leaders. The purpose of the meeting was to analyze the future of the U.S. information technology industry between 1997-2002. Besides Jones International, participants included representatives of the global telephone industry, banking, computer manufacturers and software, carriers and network equipment companies.

A note of explanation is important here. NCRI has pioneered a hybrid form of scenario development called Future Mapping, using "endstates." Unlike most scenario consultants, who let their clients assemble driving forces, analyze and then write original scenarios, NCRI's tactic is to assemble a deep database of its own that permeates a particular company or industry, then the principals and staff of NCRI write the primary scenarios/endstates *prior to the scenario building exercise with the clients*. The clients are informed of the scenarios/endstates in advance, given a chance to choose the particular scenario analysis group they want to join, then are presented with the extensive database of facts which led up to all of the scenarios. The clients are challenged to add to each scenario, come up with their own variations, and also explain some of the ramifications of the scenarios.

It is a more regimented form of scenario development than is often practiced by firms such as Global Business Network or Coates & Jarratt, and is more outcome-focused than the others, which often revel in the process itself. It works very well because it is factual, NCRI's staff understands their focus industries and due to the importance of documented data. NCRI's approach can respond to highly volatile technology-based shifts and conditions that tend to dominate today's high technology environment.

Future Mapping also allows strategic planning managers to immediately deploy the results of the scenarios into their short and long-term strategic plans, often without having to defend their rationale, since these particular cases are based on current and past real time facts as much as they are on envisioning the future. In many ways, Future Mapping seems to be an adaptation of some Delphi-style analysis techniques used in strategic plans, laid up against the need to have some type of template to analyze a horizon that, in the technology world, is moving toward us at an ever-accelerating rate.

The defining question for our NCRI group was, "How will the U.S. computing and communications markets evolve in the period 1997-2002?" The following summary of the results of the process are reprinted with the permission of NCRI:[56]

The four prevailing scenarios, or "endstates" which the two-day scenario process (there were two scenario groups, one met on the West Coast and the other on the East Coast) analyzed were:

Endstate A — Volume Drivers

Volume, such as that generated by the WinTel duopoly, is the key to success and profitability. One or two players dominate each major sector of the industry. Users embrace these volume leaders as the *de facto* standards and praise their interoperability and ease of use.

Endstate B — Internet Wins

The Internet/Web has become the common application platform throughout the industry. Electronic commerce flourishes, and new ways of doing business proliferate as the Web enables easy information sharing and interoperability. The Web evolves into a new consumer medium.

Endstate C — Vertical Solutions

The ongoing spiral of complexity and innovation forces users to rely on integrators and VARs to make it all work. Vertical-industry knowledge and deep technology expertise are keys to success.

A large-scale application of information technology (IT) to gain competitive advantage becomes a type of industrial arms race.

Endstate D — Service Utilities

The Internet service providers (ISPs) and carriers take center stage with packaged service utilities bundling desktops, servers, and networks together. The success of thin-client computing and network-centric hosting enables the rapid adoption of this new services model.

These "endstates" led to some fairly powerful conclusions which are already finding their way into corporate strategies:

- Rapid and widespread acceptance of electronic commerce driven by reductions in the cost of doing business.

- The Web will be the dominant user interface for all types of applications and information access.

- The end of the operating system wars; although there is a general belief that UNIX will be squeezed by NT at the low end and CMOS OS/390 IBM mainframe technology at the high end, the groups generally did not believe that the OS is any longer a critical path item, thanks to the ability of the Web and Java to mask the OS and create a platform that spans OSs.

- Re-centralization of data management and operations due to cheap networking, adoption of a thinner client and more server centric software architecture, and users' desire to achieve higher economies of scale and deliver more reliable operations.

- Near-term and widespread availability and acceptance of Internet security solutions for transaction processing and content protection.

- Near ubiquitous availability of affordable broadband services to home and business in developed countries.

- Rapid network performance improvement outstripping continued computing performance improvements for the foreseeable future.

- Rapid spread and market acceptance of virtual workgroups and virtual application utilities operated by network-based third parties. An example of a virtual application utility might be a network-based version of PeopleSoft based on servers, with related support operated by ADP (Automated Data Processing) and made available to corporate customers on a monthly leased basis via remote network access to the ADP PeopleSoft servers.

Given that the majority of the participants represent major industry suppliers, it is not surprising that they are upbeat about the potential for new technologies to transform existing markets and create new ones. Nonetheless, it is striking how compelling the groups find the market pull of the Internet, and how strongly they believe in the ability of customers to rapidly adjust their buying behaviors and vendor loyalties.

In terms of discontinuities between the two groups, thoughts on the role of network computers (NCs) varied. The West Coast included a group of strong NC supporters who see the NC as the way to drive volume sales and rapidly extend participation in cyber markets. In general, the West Coast group believed more strongly in consumer market drivers and their ability to influence the overall behavior of the market. The East

Coast group looked more toward the corporate user community as the market motivators.

What became immediately apparent to most of the participants was that the scenario concerning the ubiquity of the Internet was becoming true almost as fast as the scenarios could be written, reviewed, and released on the same media that the group was trying to divine.

In cases like this, a version of Free Market Fusion — the privatization of the government and academic research-spawned Internet industry — occurred with an accelerated and mind-numbing velocity.

Appendix B — Education and Community: Four Scenarios for the Future of Public Education

These scenarios were summarized, with permission, from a report on a 1994 scenario project conducted by the Global Business Network (GBN), a scenario consulting firm based in Emeryville, California. GBN conducted the project for the National Education Association (NEA), one of its clients.[57] Unlike most of GBN's scenario development projects, it is not proprietary. Edited down as they are, there are some leaps and discontinuities in the following text. For the full text of the original report, go to GBN's Web site at http://www.gbn.org. Education is a concern of everyone, but it is one of those issues that runs the risk of being everyone's problem, therefore no one's problem.

Author's Note:

For the aspiring entrepreneur, take special note of Scenario 3 which deals with a highly technology-enabled public education system. The opportunities for products and services are clearly spelled out and provide an excellent example of how scenario exercises can identify Free Market Fusion opportunities. (That discussion is continued in the final sections on the implications for all of the scenarios.)

Why Public Education Scenarios?

Education is a big industry. The U.S. spends approximately 7.5 percent of its GDP on education; in 1994 it spent some $275 billion on public K-12 education alone. But education isn't run like a business. Something about education seems to resist replication. Faced with this dilemma, and others equally daunting, the National Education Association (NEA) and Global Business Network (GBN) engaged in a project to develop scenarios for the future delivery of public education in the U.S.

Scenario planning is more process than product, as this project clearly demonstrates. This report captures only a small portion of the strategic conversation that contributed to the current state of these scenarios. As is often the case in scenario planning, the scenarios have evolved. Following a brief section on what scenarios are and are not, the core framework for the scenarios will be presented.

The four scenario narratives follow, and the report concludes by discussing the implications of these scenarios.

In an earlier workshop on the future of urban education, the staff of the NEA Pacific Region concluded that urban reform was a necessary if not sufficient condition of urban educational reform. A good many of the failings of urban education today can be laid at the doorstep of failing families and failing urban communities.

Consider some statistics from the Carnegie Corporation report on the state of children (*The New York Times*, April 12, 1994):

	1960 %	1990 %
Children born to unmarried mothers	5	28
Children under 3 living with one parent	7	27
Children under 3 living with both parents	90	71
Children under 18 living in a one-parent family	10	21

Special Education and Inclusion

To appreciate this resonance between the axes of our scenario matrix and one hotly-debated educational issue, consider the controversial topic of inclusion: the practice of including special education students in regular classrooms — a very real testing ground for the ideals of inclusive community.

Among the most strongly worded of its recommendations in Rediscovering Education: Creating Schools for the 21st century (February 1994), we find:

Special Education/Inclusion is clearly a thorny issue.

Special ed. classes are being used to shunt some minority students out of regular classes where they might get a better education.

Technology and Education

The information revolution is coming to education. P. Kenneth Komoski, executive director of the Educational Products Information Exchange Institute, suggests that we use technology to restructure our schools and communities for lifelong learning:

In the course of a year, kids spend only 19 percent of their potential learning time in school.

The largest segment of the 81 percent of kids' outside-of-school time is the well-documented 25 percent they devote to TV watching and video-game playing.

The vision is one of locally managed, community-wide, people-driven electronic networks for learning and information that are designed by and for local citizens to reflect their own needs. Educational networks can enhance community development. Bob Hughes, Boeing's corporate director of education relations, looks to computer networks as a key to turning out students who adapt readily to change and who solve problems by seeking out and applying new ideas.

Scenario 1, entitled Orthodoxy, represents a highly centralized, conservative picture of education. By contrast, Scenario 2, Orthodoxies, depicts a world of many small, relatively autonomous communities. Scenario 3, Wired for Learning, describes a highly privatized, high-technology education environment. Finally, Scenario 4, The Learning Society, describes a relatively optimistic education scenario in a healthy economy.

This scenario development group spent as much (if not more) time trying to understand the potential directions that American society might take as it did inquiring into possible directions for American education. This is understandable, because our system of education is indissolubly rooted in the nature of our society. Major shifts in social attitudes and organization will have profound effects on our system of education. To reflect this concern, a major portion of each scenario looks at developments in society itself.

Scenario I — Orthodoxy

The time: 2005. Education is also about building character and proper respect for authority.

Also, while the civil rights movement erased some of the blatant political differences among America's peoples, increasingly glaring economic differences remain. Ethical values take precedence over economic value-added; virtues are more valued than virtual reality. Higher education has become both more expensive and less able to meet student and labor market demands. Within the K-12 sector, the explosion of students with special needs, the growth of ethnic and linguistic diversity within the student population, and the increase of on-campus violence has turned many schools into hostile environments. Schools suffer their own complex versions of the physical infrastructure crisis: Leaky roofs, inadequate mechanical and electrical systems, and crumbling bricks and mortar combine to make many schools unattractive and unsafe.

America has a mixed history in managing diversity. For all the lip service paid to social and political equality, large opportunity and economic achievement gaps exist among its many racial and ethnic groups.

The social and economic crisis hit at the very legitimacy of the American political system and way of life. New conservative forces sought to gain influence over political institutions. By the time of the crisis, the free market approach to social problems was largely discredited in popular political discourse.

Features of a National Education System:

Federal Control

The magnitude of the economic crisis demands that the federal government mobilize its resources to come to the aid of education.

A National Curriculum

While many students are capable of mastering the skills at the middle levels, few attain the highest levels. The curriculum redesign project is orchestrated at the federal level and implemented without much alteration in different states and school districts. Education and training are linked closely together. Students are encouraged to develop skills that are expected to be in demand in the future.

National standards make it abundantly clear which students, and which schools, are succeeding and failing. When individual students compete against students from other schools and localities for federally funded scholarship dollars, individuals' scores are adjusted by a factor based on their respective school scores, so students from districts with weak school systems are not penalized or unduly advantaged by their local school system.

National standards combined with information technology have introduced a new transparency into evaluation: grades are no longer given to students alone, but to teachers, schools, and entire school districts.

Information Technology and the State

In the case of learning-disabled and slower students, the technologies are used primarily as electronic workbooks. Critics of the government suggest that the latter use of technology is disproportionately reserved for disadvantaged students.

Many today feel that the impact of information technologies would have been far greater if the federal government had not taken such a controlling role in education. The curriculum severely circumscribes the ability of individual schools and teachers to choose subject matter and materials. People need skills, and information technology, combined with strict norms, serves to inculcate those necessary skills.

Economic inequality correlates closely with levels of educational attainment. Will education become indoctrination?

Scenario 2 — Orthodoxies

Like the last scenario, this one, too, plays out the reaction against value-free public education. Today's public education would seem to avoid imposing any one set of values in order to avoid offending other sets of values. Here, values are also central to education, but different values guide different schools.

The Diverse Society

The changing racial and ethnic proportions within the general population have created fissures within the larger society.

The American political system has reinforced these movements by granting "new towns" a high degree of political and fiscal autonomy, just as charter schools were granted waivers from the regulations that had governed the public school system. Outside traditional political institutions, new town associations have organized their own multi-association congresses to deal with social service problems. Education has become increasingly private or parochial.

Characteristics of the Educational Mosaic:

Curricular Differences

Schools in this period function as the centers of their communities. There are Baptist schools, Catholic schools, Vietnamese schools, schools for the children of ecologically conscious parents, and schools for the very affluent.

As one would expect, children in Vietnamese schools learn about Vietnamese history alongside U.S. history. As with other ethnocentric communities, cultural training is very important.

Overwhelmingly secular, these schools offer rigorous training in all traditional subjects and a wide range of electives.

Communities of environmentally concerned citizens (so-called "eco-communities") stress instruction in the relationship of human beings to the world around them. Each community establishes its own truth. American society and its schools have collectively created many different truths. In spite of apparently enormous curricular differences, most schools focus on the same familiar core of academic subjects: reading, literature, history, science, mathematics, and social studies. A certain degree of uniformity among the enormous number of local educational systems can be attributed to the admissions requirements for higher education, which draws its students from a wide variety of backgrounds. In deference to the aspirations of parents for their children, local schools place a great deal of emphasis on preparing students in these areas.

Well-funded schools are able to purchase state-of-the-art materials and pay the best teachers more easily than poorly funded schools. Because education has largely become a private-sector institution, there is little regulation of educational programs and services. Private rating services provide studies of educational quality for parents, property associations, and municipalities.

In order to deal with funding inequities while honoring the autonomy of new towns, some states have levied taxes on gated communities to raise funds for public municipalities. Other states offer tax rebates for those willing to attend school outside of their communities.

Types of Schools

Some schools today are privately owned and operated by new town associations or parent organizations. In other situations, education is a combination of cottage industry for local residents and investment opportunity for a growing number of private corporations. To enhance their market share, many companies offer programs targeted at specific social groups.

On the one hand, schools can readily implement changes in the curriculum and the organization of the school if they choose. There is no faceless bureaucracy at the community or state level to object to changes. Some of the larger corporations seek to deal with this problem by organizing their own schools, which reflect the diversity of their workforces.

Scenario 3 — Wired for Learning

This scenario revolves around new applications of information technology. As described in the introductory section on predetermined elements, information technology will influence all of the scenarios. But this scenario is distinguished by an evolution of information technology more rapid and far-reaching than most people now anticipate. That info-tech will influence education is predetermined. This scenario assumes that the evolution is very fast, and that information technology is the biggest story in the transformation of education over the next decade.

Some people, representing both eastern and western orthodoxies, just don't like the heavy reliance on information technology that has overtaken education.

Some companies market services which help individuals create the unique configurations that serve their needs. But more often, popularly available software and information services permit individuals to customize their own use of information. The individual reigns in the information kingdom. People participating in the new information economy come to expect highly individualized approaches to their needs. Just as the healthcare industry went through a major transformation from a heavy dependence on hospitals to a greater reliance on outpatient clinics and ambulatory care, so the information revolution got students out of school buildings and into communities where their portable electronic devices carried a steady two-way stream of education and learning.

Characteristics of the Learning Industry:

The Education Producers

Two information giants, All Media and United Telecommunications Technologies are both heavily involved in the education market. Education draws on the companies' combined resources in software development, video production and delivery, telecommunications services, and information storage and retrieval.

Interactive distance learning courses are the specialty of Distance Technologies and its subsidiary, PacSat College. Digital Education concentrates on the design of specialized software for helping students with specific learning disabilities. For young and old students who learn best in highly interactive formats, Comcon Systems offers a range of computer and videoconferencing services. Although many of the companies involved in education have a national presence, the highly diverse education market has left room for small, local companies that address specific local needs or have ties to the communities in which they are located.

The initial boost given by the failure of the public school system has been exhausted. The economics of education are beginning to improve, thanks to productivity gains resulting from educational technology. Many educational products and services are delivered and used in a network environment.

Companies with strong presence in this market include Sylvan Learning Centers and Wayzata Experiences (a suburban Minneapolis company).

The Products

Private educational efforts in the late twentieth and early twenty-first centuries represent the rise of science-based education. For the most part, however, the education market demands products that reflect solid research into human and cognitive development. For adults, skill development for new jobs or new job responsibilities is the big market. Education companies battle vigorously in the marketplace to turn out products and courses that permit effective and convenient training. For example, when demand for high-level information skills took off following the conversion of major library collections into hypermedia databases, education companies responded with elaborate tutorials and programs on information retrieval and processing. Retrieval, not delivery, is the operative word for the new education services.

The Education Consumer

The consumer dominates education. No longer principally dependent upon a single source of education services, consumers look to schools and on-line services that may better serve their needs. Individual EdCred accounts are simply debited by learning companies when products and services are received. If a parent misspends his EdCreds on a child's education, there is no agency to turn to for a second chance. Companies with an investment in childhood education have a leg up on the competition when the expansion of education occurs. They are able to use the same infrastructure and skills to produce a new range of products focused on higher education, job skills, and cultural enhancement.

The Learning Environment

Often, however, students work at home or in neighborhood centers with on-line services, desktop videoconferencing, computer conferencing, and advanced software.

At the bottom of the labor market, temporary, part-time, and low-paid work has been abundant.

The education market has been created, but, like other markets at other times, it is imperfect. This would not be so troubling if education were not so central to a just and equitable information society. Reactions to this scenario included the usual awe at gee-whiz technology, but misgivings about inequality of access given the premise of exclusive electronic communities. This scenario plays out the emphasis on computation.

Scenario 4 — The Learning Society

In this scenario the pieces come together. Technology moves faster than in the first two scenarios, making this a radical change scenario. But the technology serves the ideals of inclusive community by facilitating a more participatory process than in the last scenario. Technology is a tool, not a driver. The marketplace is less central than public space. While every bit as ubiquitous as in Wired for Learning, technology fades into the background of The Learning Society.

The Search for Community

Parents drop off at daycare, the neighbor's house, or school. Many others lack the time and financial resources to take care of their own needs and those of their children.

Children rarely see their parents. Many people lose contact with their neighbors. Even for those who do not need financial help, the growth of new forms of community provide much-needed points of contact with the larger society. America begins to tap into its true reservoir of resources — its people.

With resources stretched thin, the social fabric often needs mending. Electronic networks create new forms of community, permitting congenial and convenient ways of meeting on-line. Unlike earlier immigrant communities and ethnic enclaves, communities in this period thrive on diversity. School curricula encourages students to understand and respect one another. Children are taught strategies for managing aggression. Within communities, members learn how to solve their conflicts peacefully.

America is growing together again

Government by objective replaces government by prescription. Federal and state governments make substantial investments in physical infrastructure. Government's emphasis on capacity-building is perhaps greatest in the areas of education and training.

Public Education for All

America's role in the global economy has grown. Information technology companies lead the world in supercomputers, chip technology, and flat-panel displays. The long-standing problem that precipitated the reform of American education was the challenge of creating a high-skill workforce. The economic rise has created a voracious demand for those with university and postgraduate training, as well as for high school graduates with higher-level skills in mathematics, the sciences, and abstract reasoning. The community needs a public education system with the depth to treat each student as a client, the foresight to provide training relevant to tomorrow's labor market, and enough sensitivity to cultural issues that tolerance and respect for all peoples is taught.

The collective wisdom of teachers, parents, and members of our community is essential to resolving the issues brought forth in this scenario.

Decentralization and Educational Diversity

As with so many educational movements, it starts in the states. Districts deduct a pro rata share of each school's share of the district's overhead and pass the rest on to the schools. Purchasing, curriculum development, and a wide range of policy decisions were made by teaching professionals at the school site. Responsibility for setting the overall direction of schools belonged to governing councils of teachers and parents. New data communications networks allow teachers instant access to on-line help. Some offer help for students with specific cognitive disabilities. There are schools for foreign language training, schools for music, and schools for science. Schools experiment with schedules, opening and closing at different times for the convenience of students and parents. Schools have begun to use increasingly sophisticated public data networks to deliver instruction and counseling to students in their homes. Learning can be distributed to individual students at multiple sites, while many students can access the same on-line resources at the same time. Boundaries blur: the bricks and mortar of the school building cease to bound education in space, and K-12 ceases to bound education in time as pre-kindergarten and lifelong learning become portable for all. More funds can be spent directly on education.

Although considerable discretion exists at the school site, the state of California ensures that the overall system works through what amounts to a public education marketplace. Increasingly sophisticated standards and assessment systems permit close tracking of education programs. Parents are free to choose which schools their children attend. Guidelines are published and widely distributed that show future labor market projections and highlight individual school efforts. To make sure the information reaches everyone, special Department of Education employees fan out into non-English-speaking communities to share this information with parents.

In many areas of the country, public schools now serve as community centers. For K-12 students, they integrate social services with educational offerings. A growing number now offer learning options that extend from pre-kindergarten education to life-enrichment programs for senior citizens. State and federal support for lifelong learning activities is now commonplace. As new functions have been added, schools have changed physically. Many now incorporate senior centers, pre-kindergarten programs, adult training, and K-12 education under one roof. Senior citizens, for example, have become an increasingly valuable resource to the school community.

Likewise, students have been able to offer adults help with using new technologies.

So much needs to happen outside education in order for this scenario to unfold: rapid evolution of information technology, a fundamental change in values, a new thirst for community.

What can educators do by themselves to promote these changes that will in turn change education?

Implications of these Scenarios:

The Role of Values in Education

The first two scenarios, Orthodoxy and Orthodoxies, represent worlds driven by a dissatisfaction with value-free or value-neutral education.

Looking at the set of scenarios as a whole, values play a critical role for communities apart; and Learning Society is driven by a transformation in values leading to the revaluing of community. Some values are better than no values. And education is incomplete without any values at all.

Information Technology

Wired for Learning may not be the scenario most preferred by most teachers. It is, as just mentioned parenthetically, the scenario least driven by values. Nonetheless it would be a mistake to imagine that information technology is absent from the other three scenarios. Information technology advances in those other scenarios as well, just not as fast or as much in the foreground.

Bridge-Building

Other implications for educators can doubtless be drawn from these scenarios. Turning from the implications of these scenarios for the NEA and public education, what are their implications for other World View organizations and global corporations in general? Quite independent of the questions of values, technology, or connections with communities, these scenarios pose a challenge to industry: Where are your workers and consumers going to come from? Precisely because these scenarios challenge any easy confidence in the future of public education, they raise problems for marketers and human resource executives. Public education is everyone's problem, whether public or private and therefore risks being no one's problem. If community and education are as closely linked as these scenarios suggest, then the community that includes all sectors, companies, private schools and public schools, must come to recognize the web of mutual responsibilities that binds private corporations to the education process.

Author's Comment:

Education scenarios as a field of study offer an infinite range of possibilities. Global Business Network's scenarios were composed in 1994 with a focus on the California public education K-12 system. New and different scenarios can be constructed using parties from the private sector and the world's higher education institutions.

One sure trend to be explored with this type of planning and brainstorming is the impact of private involvement in the actual delivery of education at all levels in the 21st century. This type of cooperative planning process is essential to examining new possibilities for education delivery that may help traditional education interests and private sector groups develop an enlightened understanding of one another's interests and aspirations for education.

We must beware of the possibility of constructed scenarios that are "pre-premised." They reach conclusions desired by their participants for the purpose of supporting their public relations, marketing, self justification or fundraising efforts. Clearly, such scenarios are of little help in the Free Market Fusion process. Accordingly, premises should be examined for objectivity in reviewing scenarios of others but especially when you are doing your own. – GRJ

END NOTES

Introduction

[1] Alan Walters, *A Dictionary of Economics*, The New Palgrave, Vol. 2, 1987, page 422-427

[2] George Santayana, *The Life of Reason, Vol. 1, Reason and Common Sense*, New York: Charles Sons, 1905, 1906

Chapter 1

[3] Letter to Samuel Kercheval, July 12, 1816 in *Thomas Jefferson Writings*, New York: The Library of America, 1984, p. 1401

[4] Peter Drucker, *Management: An abridged and revised version of Management: Tasks, Responsibilities, Practices*, London: Pan Books Ltd., 1979, p. 151

[5] David Birch, Anne Haggerty, and David Parsons, *Who's Creating Jobs?*, Cambridge, MA: Cognetics, Inc., 1997. Birch made news when he reported, in his book *Job Generation in America*, New York: Free Press, 1987, that small businesses created 8 out of 10 new jobs in America during the period of time he studied.

Chapter 2

[6] Alvin Toffler, *Future Shock*, New York: Random House, 1970, p. 161

[7] Interview with Alvin Toffler, July 2, 1998

[8] For a history and overview of computers, see *The Age of Intelligent Machines*, by Raymond Kurzweil, Cambridge, Mass.: MIT Press, 1990

[9] David Waltz, The Prospects for Building Truly Intelligent Machines, *Daedelus*, Winter 1988, p. 204

[10] U.S. Department of Commerce. International Trade Administration. *U.S. Industrial Outlook 1993*. Washington, D.C.: Government Printing Office, 1993, p. 18-5

[11] This information was compiled from railroad timetables in the Western History Collection at the Denver Public Library

[12] James W. Carey, *Communications as Culture: Essays on Media and Society*, Boston: Unwin Hyman, 1989, p.223-7

[13] Carey, *Communication as Culture*, p. 201

[14]Quoted in Carey, *Communication as Culture*, p. 182

[15]Toffler, *Future Shock*, p. 249

[16]*NUA Internet Surveys*, http://www.nua.ie, December 17, 1998

[17]"Pricing the Net," *The Economist*, October 19, 1996: p. 23

Chapter 3

[18]Richard Saul Wurman, *Information Anxiety*, New York: Bantam Books, 1990, p. 206

[19]Alvin Toffler, *Powershift: Knowledge, Wealth and Violence at the Edge of the 21ˢᵗ century*, New York: Bantam Books, 1990

[20]Garry Wills, *Certain Trumpets: The Nature of Leadership*, New York: Simon & Schuster, 1994, p.125-126

[21]Wills, *Certain Trumpets*, p.131

[22]The first cable systems in the U.S. were founded, separately, in 1948 by Ed Parsons in Astoria, Oregon, and John Walson in Mahanoy City, Pennsylvania. In the late 1940s, these two individuals (and possibly others) at opposite ends of the country started stringing cable to deliver clearer television signals to residents in remote communities, thereby starting an industry that would grow up to revolutionize not only television transmission, but the nature of television itself.

[23]For a history of Home Box Office, see Inside HBO: *The Billion Dollar War between HBO, Hollywood, and the Home Video Revolution*, by George Mair, New York: Dodd, Mead & Company, 1988

[24]*Cablevision*, February 9, 1998, p. 42

[25]*The Kagan Media Index*, Paul Kagan Associates, May 27, 1998, p. 8

[26]Estimating the Home-Schooled Population," Washington, D.C.: Office of Research, Department of Education, 1991, p. 4, Document No. ED337903

Chapter 4

[27]David Osborne and Ted Gaebler, *Reinventing Government: How the Entrepreneurial Spirit is Transforming the Public Sector*, Reading, Mass.: Addison-Wesley, 1992, p. 30; also, see

David Osborne and Peter Plastrik, Banishing Bureaucracy: *The Five Strategies for Reinventing Government*, Reading, Mass.: Addison-Wesley, 1997

[28]Bernard Wysocki Jr., "For This Economist, Long Term Prosperity Hangs on Good Ideas," *The Wall Street Journal*, January 21, 1997, page A1

[29]Marvin Cetron and Owen Davies, *American Renaissance: Our Life at the Turn of the 21st century*, New York: St. Martin's Press, 1989, p. 63

Chapter 5

[30]Neil Baldwin, Edison, *Inventing the Century*, Hyperion, New York, 1995; p.71

[31]U.S. Department of Commerce, Bureau of the Census, *Statistical Abstract of the United States 1997*, Washington, D.C.: http://www.census.gov/prod/3/97pubs/97statab/business.pdf, tables 852, 861, and 862

[32]*U.S. Statistical Abstract*, 1995, p.556

[33]Milton Friedman, *Capitalism and Freedom*, Chicago:University of Chicago Press, 1962

[34]In *CNN: The Inside Story*, Boston: Little, Brown, pp. 104-105, Hank Whittemore offers readers some wonderful conventional wisdom that circulated as Ted Turner struggled to get his "lean, mean, and hungry" enterprise on the air:

> *It certainly is an interesting idea, but the question is how they'll execute it. I don't think people want to just watch some guy rip and read the news off the wires. But once you start moving crews into hot spots, the money's heavy. On a big story, say in Cuba or Iran, you might have to send two or three crews. One trip like that and you could feed a family of four for a year.* — Burton Benjamin, Vice President and Director of CBS News

> *Each of the three commercial networks, whose service I am sorry to say is a great deal less than twenty-four hours a day, is spending around $100 million, this year, to cover news. Turner has allocated less than a fourth of that amount. And there's the rub.* — Richard Salant, NBC Board Vice-Chairman

Post-Newsweek formed some conclusions about the realities of the marketplace. The reason Ted Turner decided to go ahead with it, in the form that he's doing, may be that he doesn't understand the problem. He's not paying attention. — J. Christopher Burns, Vice President, Washington Post Co.

We run through that [CNN's $30 million annual budget] in two or three months. — Roone Arledge, ABC News Director

Why would anybody choose to watch a patched-together news operation that's just starting against an organization like ours that's been going for fifty years and spends $100-$150 million a year? — Bill Leonard, President of CBS News

[35]Joseph Schumpeter, *Capitalism, Socialism, and Democracy*, New York: Harper Torchbooks, 1976, p. 132

[36]James Fallows, *More Like Us: Making America Great Again*, Boston: Houghton Mifflin, 1989, p. 200

[37]Fallows, *More Like Us*, p. 27

[38]James Fallows, *Looking at the Sun: The Rise of the New East Asian Economic and Political System*, New York: Pantheon Books, 1994, p. 5

[39]James Fallows, "How the Far East was won", *U.S. News and World Report*, December 8, 1997, p. 11

[40]Alexis de Tocqueville, *Democracy in America*, New York: Harper Collins, 1988 p. 404

Chapter 6
[41]Miyamoto Musashi, *A Book of Five Rings: The Classic Guide to Strategy*, New York: The Overlook Press, 1974, p. 49

Chapter 7
[42]Peter Schwartz, *The Art of the Long View: Planning for the Future in an Uncertain World*, 1991, 1996, New York: Currency Doubleday, pp. 3-4

[43]Adam M. Brandenburger and Barry J. Nalebuff, "The Right Game: Use Game Theory to Shape Strategy," *Harvard Business Review*, July-August 1995, p.58

[44]Stephen Hawking, "The Future of the Universe," in *Predicting the Future*, edited by Leo Howe and Alan Wain, Cambridge: Cambridge University Press, 1993, p. 8-9

[45]David Mercer, *Scenarios Made Easy*, Abstract on the Internet,http://elsa.dmu.ac.uk/~elsa/GASS/lrp/000155/00000155.html

[46]David Mercer, *Scenarios Made Easy*

[47]Michel Godet, *Scenarios and Strategic Management*, London: Butterworths, 1987

[48]Art Kleiner, *The Age of Heretics: Heroes, Outlaws, and the Forerunners of Corporate Change*, New York: Currency/Doubleday, New York, 1996, p. 204-214

[49]Theodore Modis, *Predictions: Society's telltale Signature Reveals the Past and Forecasts the Future*, New York: Simon & Schuster, 1992, pp. 13-14

[50]Modis, *Predictions*, p. 13-14

[51]Schwartz, *The Art of the Long View*, p. 7

[52]Schwartz, *The Art of the Long View*, p. 108, 113-114

[53]Schwartz, *The Art of the Long View*, p. 103, 108

[54]Joseph F. Coates, "Scenarios Part Two: Alternative Futures," in *Nonextrapolative Methods in Business Forecasting: Scenarios, Vision and Issues Management*, edited by Jay S. Mendell, Westport: Quorum Books, 1985, p.24

[55]Lawrence Wilkinson, "How to Build Scenarios," *Wired Scenarios, Wired Magazine* Special Edition, Oct., 1995, p.74

Appendix A
[56]"Mapping the Future of Computing and Communications," Report by Northeast Consulting Resources, Inc., Boston, Mass., December 30, 1996, Case No. Q-7580

Appendix B
[57]Global Business Network Homepage and Scenario Bibliography, http://www.gbn.org/scenarios/NEA/NEA.html

CASE STUDY: 1

KNOWLEDGE TV AND JONES KNOWLEDGE GROUP

Mission: To provide affordable, accredited and not-for-credit adult and college level courses via TV and the Internet to adult learners around the globe.

Year founded: 1987

Partners: Jones Knowledge Group, 30 accredited U.S. colleges and universities.

Free Market Fusion dynamic: Jones companies, through existing relationships with various TV cable and satellite systems around the world, provides technology and creative expertise to its partners in order to make college-level and adult coursework available at affordable prices via TV and the Internet.

Market Need

Traditional university campuses, public or private, can't make education available to as many people as need it. They don't have the money. And, many don't have the entrepreneurial spirit needed to create innovative solutions to education delivery problems worldwide. Those solutions should be created immediately. Here are some statistics to ponder:

- There are between five million and seven million part-time higher education students in the United States alone.

- From 1978 to 1993, the number of U.S. 25 to 64 year olds attending school rose 45%.[1]

- One year's tuition at an elite private university or college in the U.S. costs about $23,000. In 2000 the cost could be as high as $40,000.[2]

- According to the American Society of Training and Development, 65% of all jobs available in the U. S. and most developed countries in the year 2000 will require some training or education beyond higher school, compared with 1995's 54%.

- By the end of the 20th century, UNESCO, the United Nation's Educational, Scientific, and Cultural Organization, predicts there could be as many as 1 billion illiterate people in the world. Today there are 900 million.[3]
- More than 100 million students across the globe drop out of school prematurely.[4]

Beyond the statistics lies the disturbing trend that most of the world's knowledge is the preserve of the most highly developed countries. Disseminating that knowledge worldwide is imperative to attain a more peaceful world; where business and industry can find the work force needed to create economic prosperity; and where individuals can have the opportunity to participate in that prosperity.

In addition, there is a worldwide teacher shortage. UNESCO estimates there may be more than 50 million teachers needed worldwide by 2000. Payment for their services represents 50% to 80% of current public education expenditures in almost all countries.[5]

The Solution

Adding courses delivered via cable TV or other electronic means to a school's offerings can provide economies of scale. A conventional course, needing a teacher and a classroom, incurs start-up costs each time it's taught. They also are limited in size. A distance course, once developed and produced, can be distributed at minimal cost to hundreds of thousands of students.

If an innovative solution incorporates a fairly non-traditional concept, often it is easier to work with a partner who already is comfortable with the non-traditional concept. For example, a group of Jones companies combined non-traditional delivery processes (cable television, satellites, computers and the Internet) with nontraditional teaching methods using highly adaptive and affordable software applied over the Internet.

The cable TV network called Knowledge TV is intended to create excitement about education and motivates viewers to view special Internet sites on their computers or call an 800 number to further their inquiry on how to pursue their educational interests.

These special Web sites and the toll-free phone number open the electronic gateway for TV viewers to become students in cyberschools or cybercampuses.

Attitude is crucial in the fusion equation. One of the companies, Jones International University is a completely Internet-based higher education institution launched in the mid-1990s. In the spring of 1999, it became the first fully accredited cyber university. *e*-education and College Connection, the university's sister organizations, provide Web-based tools and overall administrative support to other for-credit higher education institutions. The company's cable channel is a key component in the marketing, since it frequently advertises relevant Web addresses and toll-free numbers to connect to Jones IU and other universities. Thanks to cooperation and reciprocal motivation among the staff members of all enterprises involved, this is done in a manner that builds interest and excitement about the benefits of education.

Knowledge TV has made the living room a potential classroom for at least 22 million cable television subscribers in North America, plus viewers in other countries.

For distance education, television arguably has been the transforming technology of the 20th century. The opening of the ultra high frequency spectrum in the 1960s and 1970s — which brought the explosive growth of non-commercial television stations — plus the advent of cable TV, brought education programming home, so to speak. The Internet is rapidly proving to be the next technology of choice for education.

Extending the Human Mind

It was and is an entrepreneurial vision: Knowledge TV and its affiliates are in the business of extending the human mind. Knowledge TV is a proactive, entrepreneurial effort to empower the individual through education, and in that manner to contribute to the conversion of information into knowledge, understanding, and wisdom.

In November 1987, Knowledge TV began as a basic cable television channel designed to meet diverse needs for education, information, and instruction.

The network's programming originally focused primarily on for-credit telecourses in science, fine arts, English, mathematics, foreign languages, general business and computing. Knowledge TV's diverse and fairly expansive college-level programming wasn't just available for those who were working on college degrees. Anyone with cable service that provided Knowledge TV's cable channel could tune in and take advantage of well-produced, insightful educational programming from universities all over the country. It was much like sitting in on a traditional university class for no credit: You viewed the programming but didn't receive college credit unless you met certain entrance requirements, enrolled in the course, and paid your tuition.

Similarly, an Internet-delivered course can be previewed before enrolling.

How Knowledge TV Works

Knowledge TV is distributed to learners via satellite and cable technology. Its programming is transmitted by satellite to cable television systems, then by cable or satellite into students' homes or businesses, or to libraries and school classrooms.

Originally, for college-level courses, for-credit students often used videocassette recorders to tape the class, then replayed it at their convenience. This enabled them to fit coursework into their own schedules. It also gave them the opportunity to review classes to more fully understand the topics, concepts or the instructor's points. Students who missed a lesson could call the College Connection Student Support Center, and a representative sent a replacement tape immediately. That way there was as little interruption as possible in the continuity of the course.

Each month, a program schedule listing the course offerings for that period was sent to students and others who indicated interest in the telecourses. (Research indicated that that most Knowledge TV students "previewed" or watched a course at least once before enrolling in it.) Registered students received a syllabus that listed the semester's schedule of their courses. In addition, the course catalog indicated what dates a course would be offered, and gave a description of the course content, credit, and cost. Courses generally began in September, January, and May, similar to the schedule a student would expect from the traditional semester structure.

As the Internet proved itself, the for-credit courses were shifted to it and Knowledge TV's orientation moved to more generalized, but still educationally oriented, programming. It creates excitement about learning and drives interested viewers to telephone numbers and Internet sites where they can become students. Its related cyber university held the world's first full graduation in cyberspace in 1998.

Where Knowledge TV's Content Originates

Knowledge TV in its original format was essentially a public-private partnership, representing the key "A" and "B" entities that are part of the Free Market Fusion process. More than 30 universities, community colleges and other education providers across the United States broadcasted distance learning courses over the channel. Knowledge TV students took part or all, in some cases, of their degree requirements without spending time on campus.

Currently, the University of Colorado, Colorado Springs, offers two masters degrees to students worldwide through Knowledge TV affiliates. The Graduate School of Business Administration and the Graduate School of Public Affairs have combined resources to offer the only integrated MBA and MPA program available via distance learning technology. The first 18 hours of coursework is the same for both degrees.

Knowledge TV and its College Connection or *e*-education affiliates don't hand out diplomas, however. A student graduating from the University of Delaware's hotel and restaurant bachelor's degree program via Knowledge TV or its affiliates, for example, will receive his or her degree from the University of Delaware. Knowledge TV and its affiliates are the delivery method. The university, including Jones International University, providing the coursework provides the credits and degree.

Paying For A Knowledge TV Education

Knowledge TV and its affiliates are an example of how public-private partnerships can bring the best of both worlds together for the benefit of the consumer — in this case the education consumer. Students can do coursework at lower cost than if they were attending on-campus. But students utilizing Knowledge TV and its College Connection affiliates (which involves multiple public and private universities as well as Jones International University) pay only for their education, not for school-related transportation, housing, athletic or health fees, or various other costs incurred in living away from home (see the chart below).

Beyond the financial savings is the saving of something equally as precious: Time. While the rigors of success in a course are the same, cyber students don't have to spend time away from their jobs or families as do those who attend classes on campus.

The Future

In terms of using television to deliver education, Knowledge TV's function has been eclipsed by the Internet. For an interim period, it is still partially viable in its original format, but it has a very important continuing role to play in less formal education. It also helps in creating excitement about learning and in driving potential students or others seeking deeper knowledge

Two-Year Colleges 1997-98 Estimated Costs Per Semester (12 Credits)

Costs	Public	Private	Knowledge TV
Tuition and Fees	$ 751	$ 3,428	$ 1,664
Room and Board	$ 941	$ 2,272	Existing costs at home
Books and Supplies	$ 305	$ 309	$ 116
Transportation	$ 489	$ 305	Existing costs at home
Other	$ 613	$ 536	Existing costs at home
Total	$ 3,099	$ 6,850	$1,780 (plus costs at home)

Source: The College Board, New York, NY; Jones Knowledge Group

Four-Year Colleges 1997-98 Estimated Costs Per Semester for Undergraduate (12 credits)			
Costs	Public	Private	Knowledge TV
Tuition and Fees	$ 1,556	$ 6,832	$ 2,618
Room and Board	$ 2,181	$ 2,775	Existing costs at home
Books and Supplies	$ 317	$ 316	$ 229
Transportation	$ 287	$ 269	Existing costs at home
Other	$ 695	$ 522	Existing costs at home
Total	$ 5,036	$10,714	$2,847

Source: The College Board, New York, NY; Jones Knowledge Group

to 800 numbers and Web site addresses. Its affiliated products, services and institutions, including *e*-education (software allowing professors or teachers to put their courseware on the Internet); College Connection (offering registrar and other cyber support to universities and others wishing to educate in cyberspace) and Jones International University (a complete cyber university) will undoubtedly deepen and widen their business on the Internet.

[1]Gene Koretz, "The Boom in Adult Education," *Business Week*, July 10, 1995, p. 24.

[2]John Elson, "The Campus of The Future," *Time*, April 13, 1992, p. 54.

[3]Asher Deleon, "'Learning to be' in retrospect," *The Unesco Courier*, April 1996, p. 11.

[4]Ibid.

[5]Robert Bisaillon, "Schools at the crossroads," *The Unesco Courier*, April 1996, p. 26.

[6]Author unknown, "TV Viewing Soars Globally," *The Futurist*, September-October 1995.

[7]Parker Rossman, *The Emerging Worldwide Electronic University: Information Age Global Higher Education,* Westport, Connecticut: Greenwood Press, 1992), p. 139.

CASE STUDY: 2

NATIONAL DIGITAL LIBRARY

Mission: To make library resources from the Library of Congress collections more generally available to everyone, for the purpose of enlightenment and education.

Year founded: 1988 (the Library of Congress was created in 1800)

Partners and contributors included: Library of Congress, Mr. John W. Kluge, The David and Lucile Packard Foundation, Ameritech, AT&T Foundation, Bell Atlantic Corporation, Citicorp Foundation, Discovery Communications, Inc., Donaldson, Lufkin & Jenrette, Eastman Kodak Company, H.F. Lenfest, Jones Family Foundation, Glenn R. Jones, Federal Express Corporation, W.K. Kellogg Foundation, Laurance S. and Mary French Rockefeller, McCormick Tribune Foundation, Pew Charitable Trusts, Occidental Petroleum Corporation, Reuters, Bankers Trust, COMPAQ Computer Corporation, R.R. Donnelly & Sons, The Ford Foundation, The Hearst Foundation, Inc., David H. Koch Charitable Foundation, Mr. Carl H. Lindner, Lucent Technologies, NYNEX Foundation, Shell Foundation, Texaco Foundation, Hewlett-Packard Company, International Business Machines Corporation, LizardTech

Free Market Fusion dynamic: The Library of Congress has financial and technical support from corporate partners, nonprofit foundations and individuals to help design and launch an electronic version of certain portions of its collections. In its early designs, the Library of Congress took portions of collections and re-rendered them digitally on laser disc media with a simple index. The role of the private sector collaboration was to place those digitized items on a multi-user server environment so that the index and materials could be accessed by many simultaneously. In addition to the multi-user feature, the distribution gained tremendously by the use of cable television and software to allow users to access these materials and indices at great distances. This effort served as a stepping stone for the Library's programs for making those and additional materials available via the Internet, as well as consulting with other national libraries in other countries for ways to both preserve and distribute their collections. The underlying concept for the project was to allow the American people access to the collections that their tax monies support, along with the philosophy that an informed electorate is a better electorate.

Market Need

An excellent example of Free Market Fusion in action is the work being done by Dr. James Billington, Librarian of Congress, in his ongoing attempts to, as he puts it, "get the champagne out of the bottle."

The Library's progressive efforts are a continuation of a legacy stretching as far back as Egypt's Alexandria library around 230 B.C.[1] with its papyrus scrolls, up through Benjamin Franklin's 18th century Philadelphia subscription library and Andrew Carnegie's 19th century endowment of some 2,500 public library buildings.

From the moment he became the Librarian of Congress in 1987, Billington has had one over-arching vision: to make access to the vast resources of the world's most extensive library a reality for every American so that citizens could use information to improve their lives and make informed decisions.

He quickly understood two facts: that advanced communications and information technologies were the key to a broad-based, widely-accessible distribution program, and that in order to achieve his laudable — if daunting — goal, he would have to secure support and expertise beyond that of the Library's highly knowledgeable 5,000-person staff or even its $322 million annual budget.[2] Both were pressed to the limits handling the Library of Congress' nearly 100 million items (increasing at a rate of one item about every five seconds).

Billington's approach has been to accept the fact that technology costs money, and then figure out how to find (or create) the appropriate convergence point between public good and private enterprise to further the goals of a universally-accessible Library. To this end, he has encouraged American entrepreneurs to join the Library of Congress in its quest for cost-effective, state-of-the-art solutions to the nation's information needs. The National Digital Library is the culmination of this effort and the umbrella project that has grown from several digital initiatives.

The Solution

The American Memory Historical Collection (http://memory.loc.gov/amem)

LIBRARY OF CONGRESS FACTS
(1997)

- Welcomed 1.8 million users and visitors.
- Held 113,026,742 items, including:
  * 17,402,100 books in the classified collections.
  * 9,308,101 books in large type and raised characters, incunabula, monographs and serials, music, bound newspapers, pamphlets, technical reports, and other printed material
  * 86,316,541 items in the non-classified collections. These included:
    – 2,390,167 audio materials, such as discs, tapes and other recorded formats
    – 49,147,855 total manuscripts
    – 4,451,790 maps
    – 11,767,481 microforms
    – 13,156,713 visual materials, including 772,104 moving images; 11,908,937 photographs; 82,628 posters; 393,044 prints and drawings.
- Registered 569,226 claims to copyright. Answered 421,150 inquiries through the Copyright office.
- Completed 530,000 research assignments for the Congress through the Congressional Research Service.
- Conducted public tours for 65,717 general visitors.
- Circulated 23,150,000 million disc, cassette, and Braille items to more than 780,000 blind and physically handicapped patrons.
- Had more than 40 million records in computer databases and the newly opened Digital Library Visitors Center hosted almost 6,200 visitors.
- Employed a staff of 4,070 employees.
- Operated with a 1996 fiscal appropriation of $361,896,000.

Source: Library of Congress, 1998

is an example of the type of innovative program that results from such a collaboration. Dubbed "The Library of Congress on a Disk," the American Memory project was first proposed by Billington in 1988 as a means of distributing electronic access to portions of the Library's collections to libraries throughout the country.

The idea was to use computers, videodisks, compact disks, and other advanced technologies to provide a multi-media approach to the collections, which often include recorded sound, film, and photographs as well as written text. This way, students could not only search the full text of manuscripts and other documents, they could also hear folk music or jazz riffs, see a film of President McKinley making his way through his inaugural parade, or listen to Theodore Roosevelt's mother discussing her son's presidency.

Students as Testors

Because the materials of the American Memory project are digitized, students are able to download their search results directly into a word-processing or desktop-publishing program for use in their school assignments. The long-term goal is to have the American Memory project available at every public library in every community. Thanks to the rapid development and accessibility of the Internet, this goal may be attained even sooner than originally planned.

Billington has noted that the Library of Congress is not only a special repository of knowledge in Washington and the national library of the United States, it must also be an electronic pioneer for the information age and an international symbol of knowledge-based democracy. By calling on America's technology entrepreneurs to help bring information to the citizenry, Billington has been able to further the Library's

goal of "the reaffirmation of Thomas Jefferson's vision."

This collaborative approach can continue to build, often resulting in what can be called "Second-Level Fusion," wherein the result of an original Free Market Fusion undertaking starts producing secondary joint-venture projects.

The Internet became an important player here as well. The National Digital Library Project evolved from this. The National Digital Library intends to have 5 million items digitized for electronic delivery on the Internet by 2000 and has raised $45 million in private funds to do so.

Assisting in the raising of the funds was the Madison Council. The Madison Council is another example of "Second Level Fusion." A national private-sector group created to serve as the Library of Congress' primary link to the business community, the Madison Council is made up of individuals who are able to help further the goals and programs of the Library of Congress through their personal and professional resources, contacts, and expertise. As Billington has noted, "The Madison Council provides the Library with a hitherto missing link between the massive resources accumulated and sustained in Washington and business, educational and cultural enterprises scattered across the nation. Madisonians are the Library's ambassadors to other communities and institutions, and are its entrepreneurial supporters in putting Library resources to work for the nation."

This leveraging, combining the strengths of one group with those of another, enables the Library to extend its resources far beyond its normal sphere of influence, for the benefit of millions around the world.

Since its inception, the National Digital Library has begun to serve as a model for other projects. National libraries in England, several European countries and Moscow have solicited the consulting advice of Billington's staff to initiate similar public-private efforts to save precious archive materials.

Future Demands

The Library of Congress is not alone in its struggle to stay on top of humankind's increasing knowledge. By conservative estimate, the holdings of the world's major libraries are doubling in volume every 14 years.[3] No wonder the Library of Congress is in the forefront of electronic resource copyright issues. As libraries shift their focus from collection to access, electronic storage and retrieval systems will be increasingly important to even the smallest libraries. Being able to leverage off of the Library of Congress will be a dominant goal for smaller libraries that wish to remain relevant.

Putting the Library's information statistics in an even more daunting light is the geometric manner in which information is growing. Various experts state that the amount of information available to us will double every five to ten years, and will continue to double in ever decreasing time spans.

In 1998, Billington and the Library of Congress were moving in a decisive way toward more information for more people. In its latest development push, the Library is adding digitized collections and investing millions in computer access to the world's largest repository of knowledge. This world-wide

database may eventually
prove to be one of the
keystones in man's history of
recorded knowledge, rivaling
many printed sources as well
as governing and regulatory
groups in influence.

---

[1] Daniel J. Boorstin, *The Discoverers: A History of Man's Search to Know His World and Himself*, New York: Vintage Books, 1985, p. 525

[2] Library of Congress staff, July, 1998

[3] Richard Saul Wurman, *Information Anxiety*, New York: Bantam Books, 1990, p. 206

CASE STUDY: 3

International Development Enterprises (IDE)

> **Mission:** Some of the world's greatest entrepreneurs are often found among those who are struggling to survive. IDE helps families in developing nations increase their food production, incomes and quality of life.
>
> **Year founded:** 1981
>
> **Partners:** International Development Enterprises (IDE), U.S. Agency for International Development, Swiss Development Corp., Interchurch Organization for Development Cooperation, Food Industry Crusade Against Hunger, Misereor, Plan International, Ford Foundation, local entrepreneurial manufacturers and distributors, farmers, and others.
>
> **Free Market Fusion dynamic:** IDE stimulates the local private sector in developing countries to produce, distribute and sell affordable technologies to rural farmers. It establishes a free market "supply chain" by counseling local manufacturers, distributors, and retailers to make and sell hand and foot-operated irrigation pumps and other devices to help poor farmers improve their productivity. It does not subsidize costs to customers, but makes prototypes and designs available to entrepreneurs, provides training, and supervises initial marketing. Once the product chain is established, IDE withdraws and lets local entrepreneurship take over.

Market Need

Paul Polak is an entrepreneur with a social conscience. He also has a proven Free Market Fusion idea: how people can make money while doing good for themselves and their neighbors.

During his "first" career, Polak was a psychiatrist who specialized in dealing with mental health problems of the poor.

"I also traveled a lot," he explains. "And it became obvious to me that many of the mental health problems around the world were rooted in the symptoms of poverty. So, when I went through mid-life crisis and decided to make a career change, attacking one of the fundamental issues — poverty behind mental patients' situations — seemed natural."

Polak is also a successful investor and entrepreneur, having dealt with small companies and start-ups most of his adult life. He understood the difference that giving poor people a chance to help themselves, as opposed to giving handouts, can make.

"This obviously doesn't work in the middle of a war or in the aftermath of an earthquake," he says. "There will continue to be a need for direct assistance in such crises."

But in relatively stable developing countries, he pinpointed millions of farmers and manual laborers who were in poverty or on the borderline. For those individuals and their families, simple farming devices and light manufacturing have made an enormous difference in their quality of life, including mental and physical health.

According to a World Bank study, large-scale irrigation projects funded by international agencies in locations such as Asia and Africa have had disappointing results in helping farmers increase food production. Still, populations are increasing, and there is an acute need for more local food production.

The same report has placed considerable hope in small-scale technology solutions to irrigation that can be implemented on an individual level. This includes the appropriate-technology approach of IDE.

The Solution

IDE has established such market-driven projects for pump and irrigation systems, as well as for coconut processing plants, in India, Nepal, Sri Lanka, Vietnam, Cambodia, Zambia, Bangladesh, and Haiti. It does this by performing market studies in countries, then designing a product manufacturing and sales system using local manufacturers and retailers. The technology — usually pumps and plastic irrigation systems — must be affordable to the poor and capable of paying for itself within one year.

Occasionally, IDE helps set up a micro-loan program so that rural farmers can quickly purchase and begin using the technology.

The pumps normally retail for $35-$50, which represents about half of many rural farmers' income, Polak says. However, the pumps allow the farmers to double their crop production, giving them additional income with which to pay off the loans and increase their buying power.

IDE has helped establish over 115 manufacturers and thousands of distributors, retailers and installers in the countries where it operates.

In the past, IDE has also sponsored other projects, such as the manufacturer of donkey carts in Somalia, jet boats for transportation in Nepal, and nut processing and marketing in Brazil.

It operates with a headquarters staff of nine, based in Lakewood, Colorado, and about 450 employees in its field offices scattered around the world. Each country has a Country Director who is usually an expatriate. All other staff are natives of those countries, in many cases trainers or trainees who eventually will become independent players in the entrepreneurial enterprises they are helping establish.

Successes

Over 13 million treadle pumps have been sold in Asia, resulting in a new $130 million in income each year for small-scale farmers in that region.

IDE entrepreneurs are now introducing low cost, slow-drip irrigation systems to many of the same customers. Those irrigation systems provide similar productivity gains for the farmers.

In Vietnam, a coconut processing plant for which IDE provided the initial design and manufacturing advice, made a profit in its second month, provided jobs for 60 people, and moved to complete independence and local ownership in less than a year. The plant processes desiccated coconut, then packages it for export and sale in such markets as China and Nepal. "That has been an out-and-out success, and it was an industry that didn't even exist," Polak says.

How It Works

IDE's technology operating principle applies throughout the organization. The first step is to perform tests with local farmers and workers using the new technology. With their feedback and input on product design, a mass-market product is finalized. All technologies used must be made as cheaply as possible but with high quality. Technologies are produced locally using local materials. Workers and farmers are assured spare parts, and IDE provides extensive training on maintenance of equipment and products.

IDE assists in market promotion through demonstrations and information distribution (including brochures in local languages and hour-long soap operas, which are staged live and then filmed). Once the product is established, IDE fades into the background or exits completely, though it is still available for consulting.

IDE presently operates on an annual budget of $4.5 million, most derived from direct grants from such organizations as the Swiss Development Corp. and AID. Most of this money goes to individual country expenses.

The organization budgets $30,000 for each country project feasibility study. It costs another $100,000 to evaluate new technology applications, which IDE staff spends considerable effort identifying and testing.

"It's not just technology that works," says Polak. "It has to be adaptable to local manufacture so we can be sure it is affordable. Something that is down right cheap by Western standards, such as a $25,000 solar energy power system for a village, is prohibitive under our business model."

Future Prospects

IDE is presently evaluating new technologies, such as low-wattage solar energy lanterns that can help village retailers extend their shop hours and, thus, their incomes. Such devices can also help improve literacy by giving children and adults the chance to study and read after sundown. Another project under study is production of low-cost bicycles.

IDE plans to expand its irrigation projects to additional countries in Asia and Latin America in the coming years, with the goal of reducing poverty and improving productivity so that poor families can permanently emerge from their cycle of poverty. "With enough income, farmers can begin letting more of their children go to school for more years," says Polak. "They also have a way to begin buying medicines and basic implements that improve their daily lives. It doesn't take much, by Western standards, to make a revolutionary difference."

IDE treadle pump in action in Bangladesh.

INDEX